SAFEGUARDING PRIVACY AND CIVIL LIBERTIES WHILE KEEPING OUR SKIES SAFE

HEARING

BEFORE THE

SUBCOMMITTEE ON TRANSPORTATION SECURITY

OF THE

COMMITTEE ON HOMELAND SECURITY HOUSE OF REPRESENTATIVES

ONE HUNDRED THIRTEENTH CONGRESS

SECOND SESSION

SEPTEMBER 18, 2014

Serial No. 113–86

Printed for the use of the Committee on Homeland Security

Available via the World Wide Web: http://www.gpo.gov/fdsys/

U.S. GOVERNMENT PUBLISHING OFFICE

93–366 PDF   WASHINGTON : 2015

For sale by the Superintendent of Documents, U.S. Government Publishing Office
Internet: bookstore.gpo.gov Phone: toll free (866) 512–1800; DC area (202) 512–1800
Fax: (202) 512–2104 Mail: Stop IDCC, Washington, DC 20402–0001

COMMITTEE ON HOMELAND SECURITY

MICHAEL T. McCAUL, Texas, *Chairman*

LAMAR SMITH, Texas
PETER T. KING, New York
MIKE ROGERS, Alabama
PAUL C. BROUN, Georgia
CANDICE S. MILLER, Michigan, *Vice Chair*
PATRICK MEEHAN, Pennsylvania
JEFF DUNCAN, South Carolina
TOM MARINO, Pennsylvania
JASON CHAFFETZ, Utah
STEVEN M. PALAZZO, Mississippi
LOU BARLETTA, Pennsylvania
RICHARD HUDSON, North Carolina
STEVE DAINES, Montana
SUSAN W. BROOKS, Indiana
SCOTT PERRY, Pennsylvania
MARK SANFORD, South Carolina
CURTIS CLAWSON, Florida

BENNIE G. THOMPSON, Mississippi
LORETTA SANCHEZ, California
SHEILA JACKSON LEE, Texas
YVETTE D. CLARKE, New York
BRIAN HIGGINS, New York
CEDRIC L. RICHMOND, Louisiana
WILLIAM R. KEATING, Massachusetts
RON BARBER, Arizona
DONALD M. PAYNE, JR., New Jersey
BETO O'ROURKE, Texas
FILEMON VELA, Texas
ERIC SWALWELL, California
VACANCY
VACANCY

BRENDAN P. SHIELDS, *Staff Director*
JOAN O'HARA, *Acting Chief Counsel*
MICHAEL S. TWINCHEK, *Chief Clerk*
I. LANIER AVANT, *Minority Staff Director*

———

SUBCOMMITTEE ON TRANSPORTATION SECURITY

RICHARD HUDSON, North Carolina, *Chairman*

MIKE ROGERS, Alabama, *Vice Chair*
CANDICE S. MILLER, Michigan
SUSAN W. BROOKS, Indiana
MARK SANFORD, South Carolina
MICHAEL T. McCAUL, Texas *(ex officio)*

CEDRIC L. RICHMOND, Louisiana
SHEILA JACKSON LEE, Texas
ERIC SWALWELL, California
BENNIE G. THOMPSON, Mississippi *(ex officio)*

AMANDA PARIKH, *Subcommittee Staff Director*
DENNIS TERRY, *Subcommittee Clerk*
BRIAN TURBYFILL, *Minority Subcommittee Staff Director*

(II)

CONTENTS

SAFEGUARDING PRIVACY AND CIVIL LIBERTIES WHILE KEEPING OUR SKIES SAFE

Thursday, September 18, 2014

U.S. HOUSE OF REPRESENTATIVES,
SUBCOMMITTEE ON TRANSPORTATION SECURITY,
COMMITTEE ON HOMELAND SECURITY,
Washington, DC.

The subcommittee met, pursuant to call, at 2:18 p.m., in Room 311, Cannon House Office Building, Hon. Richard Hudson [Chairman of the subcommittee] presiding.

Present: Representatives Hudson, Rogers, Brooks, Sanford, Richmond, Jackson Lee, and Swalwell.

Mr. HUDSON. The Committee on Homeland Security Subcommittee on Transportation Security will come to order. The subcommittee is meeting today to examine the process and procedures surrounding the U.S. Government's No-Fly and Selectee lists. I recognize myself for an opening statement.

I would like to thank our witnesses for appearing here before the subcommittee. This hearing is an opportunity to discuss how the Federal Government is working to balance civil liberties protections for U.S. citizens with the security of our aviation system.

Last week our Nation observed the 13th anniversary of 9/11. Together we remembered both the cowardly acts that took the lives of over 3,000 innocent American people and the bravery of our first responders on that tragic day. September 11 is the very reason our committee was created, and we must do everything we can to protect the homeland and prevent other attacks.

The fact remains that our enemies still view the U.S. aviation sector as a highly-attractive target, as evidenced by several thwarted plots and attempted attacks. In addition to the threats posted by al-Qaeda and its affiliates, the thousands of foreign fighters, including U.S. citizens affiliated with terrorist groups like ISIS, are a growing and serious threat to the security of U.S. aviation and the homeland. It is crucial that we accurately identify individuals who pose this threat and prevent them from boarding flights in the United States.

TSA relies on a multi-layered approach to aviation security, with everything from Federal air marshals to canines to the latest explosive detection technology. One of the these layers is a behind-the-scenes program known as Secure Flight. This program, which is the subject of today's hearing, takes passenger data it receives from airlines and matches it against the U.S. Government's consolidated terrorist watch lists, including the No-Fly and Selectee lists. This program is crucial, not only for domestic flights, but also for protecting the international flights bound for the United States.

Since 2009, TSA's Secure Flight program has evolved from one that looks solely at the No-Fly List and Selectee List maintained by the Terrorist Screening Center to one that assigns passengers a risk category and uses additional criteria to identify high-risk passengers who might not be on the watch list. While these lists serve as an important counterterrorism tool, we must ensure that travelers who are incorrectly matched to a list are able to resolve those issues in a timely, effective manner.

In two comprehensive reports issued today GAO found that TSA could improve Secure Flight by measuring and tracking errors that occur within the system and at the security screening checkpoint. The Government Accounting Office also found that TSA generally does a good job of protecting passenger data but could strengthen privacy awareness training among Secure Flight employees.

I thank the GAO for its thorough approach to examining this program, and I look forward to hearing from TSA how the agency plans to implement these Government Accounting Office recommendations.

In addition, we are pleased to have the director of the Terrorist Screening Center here today to discuss its role in managing this consolidated terrorist watch list, including the No-Fly List.

Yesterday the director of the National Counterterrorism Center, testifying before the full committee, highlighted the value of the consolidated watch list and the TSC in making sure that front-line agencies like TSA are able to identify known or suspected terrorists and stop them from entering the country, boarding an airplane, or obtaining a visa. I look forward to discussing those efforts in greater detail here today.

The bottom line is that our aviation security is only as strong as its weakest link. We must identify individuals who pose a threat, such as extremists with Western passports who have joined the fight in Iraq and Syria, and take the necessary steps to protect the homeland.

[The statement of Chairman Hudson follows:]

STATEMENT OF CHAIRMAN RICHARD HUDSON

SEPTEMBER 18, 2014

I would like to thank our witnesses for appearing before the subcommittee today. This hearing is an opportunity to discuss how the Federal Government is working to balance civil liberties protections for U.S. citizens with the security of our aviation system.

Last week, our Nation observed the 13th anniversary of 9/11. Together, we remembered both the cowardly acts that took the lives of over 3,000 innocent people and the bravery of our first responders on that tragic day. September 11 is the very reason our committee was created, and we must do everything we can to protect the homeland and prevent other attacks.

The fact remains that our enemies still view the U.S. aviation sector as a highly-attractive target, as evidenced by several thwarted plots and attempted attacks. In addition to the threats posed by al-Qaeda and its affiliates, the thousands of foreign fighters, including U.S. citizens, affiliated with terrorist groups like ISIS are a growing and serious threat to the security of U.S. aviation and the homeland. It is critical that we accurately identify individuals who pose this threat and prevent them from boarding flights to the United States.

TSA relies on a multi-layered approach to aviation security with everything from Federal Air Marshals, to canines, to the latest explosives detection technology. One of these layers is a behind-the-scenes program known as Secure Flight. This program, which is the subject of today's hearing, takes passenger data it receives from airlines and matches it against the U.S. Government's consolidated Terrorist Watch List, including the No-Fly and Selectee Lists. This program is crucial not only for domestic flights, but also for protecting international flights bound for the United States.

Since 2009, TSA's Secure Flight Program has evolved from one that looks solely at the No-Fly List and Selectee List maintained by the Terrorist Screening Center, to one that assigns passengers a risk category and uses additional criteria to identify high-risk passengers who might not be on the watch list. While these lists serve as an important counterterrorism tool, we must ensure that travelers who are incorrectly matched to a list are able to resolve those issues in a timely, effective manner.

In two comprehensive reports issued today, GAO found that TSA could improve Secure Flight by measuring and tracking errors that occur within the system and at the security-screening checkpoint. GAO also found that TSA generally does a good job of protecting passenger data but could strengthen privacy awareness training among Secure Flight employees. I thank GAO for its thorough approach to examining this program and I look forward to hearing from TSA how the agency plans to implement GAO's recommendations.

In addition, we are pleased to have the director of the Terrorist Screening Center (TSC) here today to discuss its role in managing the consolidated Terrorist Watch List, including the No-Fly List. Yesterday the director of the National Counterterrorism Center, testifying before the full committee, highlighted the value of the consolidated Watch List and the TSC in making sure that front-line agencies like TSA are able to identify known or suspected terrorists and stop them from entering the country, boarding an airplane or obtaining a visa. I look forward to discussing those efforts in greater detail here today.

The bottom line is that our aviation security is only as strong as its weakest link. We must identify individuals who pose a threat, such as extremists with Western passports who have joined the fight in Iraq or Syria, and take the necessary steps to protect the homeland.

Mr. HUDSON. The Chairman would like to point out that other Members have the opportunity to submit opening statements for the record.

[The statement of Ranking Member Thompson follows:]

STATEMENT OF RANKING MEMBER BENNIE G. THOMPSON

SEPTEMBER 18, 2014

During times of heightened security concerns, like those we currently face in light of the potential threat ISIL poses, there is a tendency to cast aside privacy concerns in favor of security at any cost. To safeguard the American public against such an overreach, it is incumbent upon this committee to review the privacy protections that the Department of Homeland Security, and its components such as the Transportation Security Administration, has in place.

Thanks to reports released today by the Government Accountability Office, we have a greater understanding of both the privacy protections and performance of TSA's Secure Flight program. This critical program helps ensure passengers designated as high-risk by the intelligence community are screened appropriately or, for those on the No-Fly list, not permitted to board a plane at all.

I look forward to hearing from our witness from the Government Accountability Office, Ms. Grover, regarding the findings and recommendations contained in the reports released today. I am also eager to hear from Mr. Sadler of TSA regarding how the agency intends to implement GAO's recommendations.

I will also be interested in hearing from TSA regarding the agency's plans to upgrade the technology used by Transportation Security Officers to better enable them to identify and ensure the proper screening of individuals designated as selectees.

The Secure Flight program is only as good as the end-user. It does no good for taxpayers to spend over $100 million a year on a program dedicated to ensuring the proper screening of individuals if Travel Document Checkers do not recognize the passengers' designation.

As it relates to current threats to aviation, I will be interested in hearing from the director of the Terrorist Screening Center about how information is obtained and used to designate individuals as selectees or to place them on the No-Fly list.

With reports of Americans having joined ISIL and other groups fighting in Syria and Iraq, our Members want assurances that individuals engaging in terrorist activities are placed on the appropriate lists in as close to real-time as possible. While Secretary Johnson was clear with the committee yesterday that there is no credible information that ISIL is planning to attack the homeland at this time, we must remain vigilant.

That means using all of the tools we have available to us to ensure that individuals who intend to commit acts of terrorism are properly identified. While doing so, we must also protect against violating the privacy and civil liberties of the American public.

In part, that means having a Constitutional appeal process for individuals wrongly designated and placed on the No-Fly List.

I look forward to hearing from both TSA and the TSC witnesses regarding how the appeal process is being revamped to address the recent decision from the 9th Circuit Court of Appeals that the previous appeals process is unconstitutional.

Mr. HUDSON. I will now introduce our distinguished panel.

Mr. Stephen Sadler currently serves as the assistant administrator for the Office of Intelligence and Analysis at the Transportation Security Administration. In this capacity, Mr. Sadler aligns intelligence functions with vetting operations and manages the technical modernization and Secure Flight mission support resources critical to the TSA mission. Mr. Sadler joined TSA in 2003 and has worked on implementing some of TSA's largest vetting and credential programs.

Mr. Chris Piehota—did I say that correctly—thank you—Mr. Piehota is the director of the Terrorist Screening Center within the Federal Bureau of Investigation. Before becoming director, Mr. Piehota served as the special agent in charge of the FBI's Buffalo field office, overseeing FBI operations in western New York from 2011 to 2013. In 2010 he joined the Terrorist Screening Center as its deputy director for operations, intelligence, and administration, and directly managed the FBI's role in the U.S. Government's 24-hour consolidated terrorist watchlisting, screening, and world-wide terrorist encounter operation enterprises.

Finally, Ms. Jennifer Grover is the acting director of the GAO's Homeland Security and Justice team, leading a portfolio of work on transportation security issues. Prior to this position, Ms. Grover was an assistant director on GAO's health care team, where she led reviews on a diverse range of health care-related issues. Ms. Grover joined the GAO in 1991.

So at this point I would like to recognize the Ranking Member, the gentleman from Louisiana, Mr. Richmond, for any opening statement that he may have.

Mr. RICHMOND. Thank you, Mr. Chairman. Thank you, Chairman Hudson, for convening this meeting today.

As the Members of this subcommittee are well aware, terrorists continue to target our commercial aviation sector for attack. Earlier this year, TSA took steps to mitigate these threats emerging from last-point-of-departure airports in Europe, Africa, and the Middle East. This past weekend, the Associated Press published an article outlining threats to commercial aviation emerging from terrorists currently residing in Syria.

Yesterday the full committee heard from the director of the National Counterterrorism Center regarding AQAP's continued pursuit of high-profile attacks against Western aviation. Today the subcommittee will examine TSA's Secure Flight program, which serves as a critical tool for identifying high-risk passengers who may pose a threat to our aviation system.

Thanks to the two Government Accountability Office reports released today, we have a clear picture of how TSA can strengthen the Secure Flight program. According to GAO, there is room for improvement in the program as it relates to both operations and privacy training for employees.

I was pleased to see that TSA referenced GAO's audits in its prepared testimony and considered the Comptroller General's feedback and recommendations invaluable. I look forward to hearing from both GAO and TSA regarding the improvements that can be made to the Secure Flight program and the time line for implementing recommended reforms.

I am also interested in hearing from the director of the Terrorist Screening Center regarding the process for placing known or suspected terrorists on the Selectee and No-Fly lists. The Secure Flight program can only be effective if the Selectee and No-Flight lists are up-to-date, accurate, and complete. For that to be a reality requires continuous collaboration between TSA, the Terrorist Screening Center, and the intelligence and law enforcement entities that nominate individuals to the watch list. Given the number of individuals known to have recently traveled to Syria and Iraq to join with terrorist groups, it is imperative that the Selectee and No-Fly lists are current and comprehensive.

In the wake of the attempted terrorist attack on Northwest Flight 253 on Christmas day in 2009, we learned valuable lessons about how TSA and CBP can better coordinate to identify potentially dangerous passengers in air transit. It is my hope that we no longer need close calls to prompt TSA to identify better ways to recognize those who pose a threat to commercial aviation.

Before yielding back, I would like to thank each of the witnesses for appearing before the subcommittee today. We appreciate what you do on a day-to-day basis to keep our Nation secure.

With that, Mr. Chairman, I yield back the balance of my time.

[The statement of Ranking Member Richmond follows:]

STATEMENT OF RANKING MEMBER CEDRIC L. RICHMOND

SEPTEMBER 18, 2014

As the Members of this subcommittee are well aware, terrorists continue to target our commercial aviation sector for attack. Earlier this year, TSA took steps to mitigate threats emerging from last point of departure airports in Europe, Africa, and the Middle East.

This past weekend, the Associated Press published an article outlining threats to commercial aviation emerging from terrorists currently residing in Syria.

Yesterday, the full committee heard from the director of the National Counterterrorism Center regarding AQAP's continued pursuit of high-profile attacks against Western aviation.

Today, the subcommittee will examine TSA's Secure Flight program, which serves as a critical tool for identifying high-risk passengers who may pose a threat to our aviation system.

Thanks to the two Government Accountability Office reports released today, we have a clear picture of how TSA can strengthen the Secure Flight program. According to GAO, there is room for improvement in the program as it relates to both operations and privacy training for employees.

I was pleased to see that TSA referenced GAO's audits in its prepared testimony and considered the comptroller general's feedback and recommendations invaluable. I look forward to hearing from both GAO and TSA regarding the improvements that can be made to the Secure Flight program and the time line for implementing recommended reforms.

I am also interested in hearing from the director of the Terrorist Screening Center regarding the process for placing known or suspected terrorist on the Selectee and No-Fly lists.

The Secure Flight program can only be effective if the Selectee and No-Fly lists are up-to-date, accurate, and complete.

For that to be a reality, it requires continuous collaboration between TSA, the Terrorist Screening Center, and the intelligence and law enforcement entities that nominate individuals to the watch list.

Given the number of individuals known to have recently traveled to Syria and Iraq to join with terrorist groups, it is imperative that the Selectee and No-Fly lists are current and comprehensive.

In the wake of the attempted terrorist attack on Northwest Flight 253 on Christmas day in 2009, we learned valuable lessons about how TSA and CBP can better coordinate to identify potentially dangerous passengers in air transit.

It is my hope that we no longer need close calls to prompt TSA to identify better ways to recognize those who pose a threat to commercial aviation.

Before yielding back, I would like to thank each of the witnesses for appearing before the subcommittee today. We appreciate what you do on a day-to-day basis to keep our Nation secure.

Mr. HUDSON. I thank the gentleman.

The full written statements from all witnesses will appear in the record.

The Chairman now recognizes Mr. Sadler for your testimony.

STATEMENT OF STEPHEN SADLER, ASSISTANT ADMINIS-TRATOR, OFFICE OF INTELLIGENCE AND ANALYSIS, TRANS-PORTATION SECURITY ADMINISTRATION, U.S. DEPARTMENT OF HOMELAND SECURITY

Mr. SADLER. Thank you, sir. Good afternoon, Chairman Hudson, Ranking Member Richmond, and Members of the subcommittee. I am pleased to be here today to talk about TSA's Secure Flight program.

The Secure Flight system was developed and implemented as a result of key recommendations in the 9/11 Commission report. Specifically, the 9/11 Commission recommended that the Federal Government assume responsibility for all watch list matching from commercial air carriers. Congress agreed, and DHS was directed to do so under the Intelligence Reform and Terrorism Prevention Act of 2004.

In 2005, Congress identified 10 conditions for this new system. Among those conditions was the establishment of a redress process for passengers who are delayed or prohibited from boarding flights. The Secretary of Homeland Security certified that all 10 conditions had been met in September 2008, and in January 2009 Secure Flight went operational.

The Secure Flight program vets more than 2.2 million passengers daily and more than 800 million travelers annually, both international and domestic, to ensure that individuals on the No-Fly List are denied boarding and that selectees are identified for appropriate screening. Secure Flight is capable of randomly selecting a percentage of passengers for additional screening to build unpredictability into the matching process.

The Secure Flight system is also critical for vetting individuals as part of TSA's risk-based security initiatives, such as the TSA PreCheck program. Intelligence-driven, risk-based security increases TSA's effectiveness by expediting the passenger screening process for known travelers while allowing us to focus our resources to those areas where we may have greater risk. We are able to more effectively mitigate risk to aviation based on the information passengers share with us ahead of time.

Additionally, the Secure Flight program has enhanced aviation security significantly by delivering earlier indication of potential matches, allowing for expedited notification of law enforcement, providing a fair and equitable and consistent matching process across all airlines, implementing critical data security protections within the Secure Flight system, and creating consistent application of an integrative redress process for misidentified individuals through the Department of Homeland Security's Traveler Redress Inquiry Program, also known as DHS TRIP.

To balance passenger privacy and security TSA has built key privacy safeguards into the Secure Flight system through administrative, operational, and technical controls to mitigate unauthorized use, disclosure, and access to information.

Two recent GAO reports on Secure Flight offer six recommendations, and TSA concurs with them all. GAO's recommendations offer us an opportunity to further ensure TSA is meeting our critical security goals. TSA strives every day to provide the most effective security in the most efficient way.

So thank you again for the opportunity to talk about this critical program. I look forward to answering your questions.

[The prepared statement of Mr. Sadler follows:]

PREPARED STATEMENT OF STEPHEN SADLER

SEPTEMBER 18, 2014

Chairman Hudson, Ranking Member Richmond, and Members of the subcommittee, I am pleased to appear before you today to discuss the Transportation Security Administration (TSA) Secure Flight program.

TSA is a high-performing counterterrorism agency charged with facilitating and securing the travel of the nearly 1.8 million air passengers each day. Our Secure Flight program is an integral layer of security, crucial to our ability to deter and prevent terrorist attacks in aviation. As you know, this system performs secure, efficient, and consistent watch list matching of passenger names for all covered domestic and international flights into, out of, and within the United States. TSA also performs these services for domestic air carrier flights between international destinations. TSA vets approximately 2.2 million passengers per day on 250 domestic and foreign carriers.

SECURE FLIGHT HISTORY

As you know, the Secure Flight program had its genesis in the 9/11 Commission Report, which recommended that TSA take over watch list matching from aircraft operators. The Intelligence Reform and Terrorism Prevention Act (IRPTA) of 2004 codified this recommendation into law, requiring DHS to conduct pre-flight comparisons of passenger information to the Terrorist Screening Database (TSDB) watch list. Prior to the implementation of Secure Flight, airlines were responsible for matching passenger information against the TSDB.

Since November 2010, Secure Flight has conducted watch list matching of passenger information against the TSDB for all covered U.S. and foreign flights into, out of, and within the United States, including point-to-point international flights operated by U.S. airlines. Secure Flight also performs watch list matching for flights that overfly, but do not land in, the continental United States.

By transferring these matching responsibilities from the airlines to TSA, Secure Flight allows for expedited notification of law enforcement, airlines, and our partners in the intelligence community to prevent individuals on the No-Fly List from boarding an aircraft, as well as ensuring that individuals on the TSDB with the "selectee" designation receive appropriate enhanced screening prior to flying. Secure Flight allows TSA and our partners in the intelligence community to adapt quickly to new threats by accommodating last-minute changes to the risk categories assigned to individual passengers. Passengers making an airline reservation are required to provide their full name, date of birth, and gender, as well as a Known Traveler Number and Redress Number, if applicable. TSA matches this information against the TSDB, then transmits the results back to airlines so they may issue or deny passenger boarding passes.

The Secure Flight program continues to evolve as TSA's approach to transportation security has shifted from a "one-size-fits-all" approach to a risk-based security approach. Improvements in technology and intelligence collection and sharing have allowed TSA to strengthen the TSA PreCheck™ program and focus our resources on individuals who may pose a higher risk to transportation security. Secure Flight is an essential component of efforts to provide population who have volunteered information about themselves such as pilots, flight attendants, members of the military, clearance holders, and individuals enrolled in Trusted Traveler programs with expedited screening. Travelers within these populations use their Known Traveler Number when making flight reservations, which allows TSA to vet them against the TSDB, confirm their eligibility for expedited screening, and provide the appropriate designation on the traveler's boarding pass.

PROGRAM ACCOMPLISHMENTS

The Secure Flight program is vital to the success of TSA's mission. Since its inception, Secure Flight has demonstrated reliability and superior effectiveness and performance compared to the aircraft operators' watch list matching abilities. Secure Flight vets more than 800 million travelers annually to ensure that individuals on the No-Fly List are denied boarding and that selectees are identified for appropriate screening.

In October 2011, TSA introduced TSA PreCheck™, a program which expedites the screening of certain known populations at the airport passenger security checkpoint, thereby enabling TSA to focus its efforts and resources on those unknown passengers. Secure Flight is critical to the operation of TSA PreCheck™. Watch list vetting and confirmation of eligibility for expedited screening are conducted by Secure Flight, which enables TSA airport staff to appropriately route and screen passengers. In December 2013, TSA expanded this program, allowing U.S. citizens and lawful permanent residents to participate via the TSA PreCheck™ Application program. Applicants undergo fingerprinting and a background investigation prior to being granted expedited screening benefits. As of August 2014, more than 500,000 individuals have applied and been successfully enrolled in the program, further allowing TSA to focus its watch list matching efforts on high-risk individuals.

Secure Flight is capable of identifying passengers flying internationally for enhanced screening measures based on risk-based, intelligence-driven information, as well as randomly selecting a percentage of passengers for additional screening to build unpredictability into the matching process. In 2013, TSA initiated TSA PreCheck™ Risk Assessments, which allows Secure Flight to enhance prescreening by utilizing intelligence-driven rule sets to identify high- and low-risk passengers, for either enhanced, standard, or expedited screening.

PRIVACY AND REDRESS

The Department of Homeland Security (DHS) integrated a robust privacy and redress system as part of the Secure Flight program. TSA has dedicated privacy staff to ensure Secure Flight systems and analyses are in compliance with applicable laws, procedures, and best practices. The system also has built-in safeguards to manage privacy risks.

TSA serves as the executive agent for the DHS Traveler Redress Inquiry Program (DHS TRIP), an interagency program made up of components of the Departments of Homeland Security, Justice, and State. It is a single point of contact for individuals who have inquiries or are looking to resolve security screening issues they have experienced during international or domestic travel, including enhanced screening, delays, or denials of boarding. These individuals can use the DHS TRIP to request redress and request that DHS, the Terrorist Screening Center which houses the TSDB, and any other involved agency review their personal information and correct their record to resolve their travel-related issues or to prevent misidentification as appropriate.

DHS TRIP has received and processed more than 185,000 redress requests and inquiries since its establishment in 2007. Once the TRIP review process is complete, and all traveler records have been updated as appropriate, DHS issues a letter to the traveler signaling the completion of the review and closure of the case. Historically, approximately 98% of the applicants to DHS TRIP are determined to be false positives. To avoid such instances, DHS TRIP assigns applicants a unique Redress Control Number, which they can use when booking travel.

Since TSA has taken over watch list matching from airlines through Secure Flight and since the implementation of DHS TRIP, DHS has seen a significant decrease in the number of redress requests.

GOVERNMENT ACCOUNTABILITY OFFICE RECOMMENDATIONS

The Government Accountability Office (GAO) has recently conducted two audits of the Secure Flight program and provided TSA with invaluable feedback through their recommendations to strengthen our systems and procedures. In their audit on Secure Flight operations, GAO recommended TSA take the following steps: Develop a process for regularly evaluating causes of screening errors, implement corrective measures based on this analysis, tie performance more effectively to program goals, and document cases to improve program performance.

TSA has already made great strides in addressing GAO's recommendations by developing data collection mechanisms to evaluate the root causes of screening errors. TSA's Office of Security Operations has taken the lead through the Security Incident Reporting Tool to collect feedback at airports including cause, corrective solution, and lessons learned from each incident. TSA expects to have this reporting system completed and implemented at all airports by the end of the month. These lessons learned will also be incorporated back into relevant program offices at TSA headquarters to ensure consistency and accountability throughout the agency.

TSA has also implemented a number of critical data security protections within the Secure Flight system, including restricting access to authorized users and requiring audit logs as well as increasing privacy training, and strengthening the approval process to allow access to data. TSA also instituted a Management Directive to manage all requests for Secure Flight data and will implement additional systems to track all data access requests.

Finally, GAO recommended that TSA develop a system to document Secure Flight system matching errors so TSA can better analyze data errors and address any matching issues in the future. Our Office of Intelligence and Analysis is developing a detailed tracking capacity for instances of system matching errors, which we expect to have completed by the end of the calendar year.

With regard to GAO's review of Secure Flight's privacy protections, TSA has already begun to incorporate their recommendations to provide privacy refresher training and to track decisions pertaining to Personally Identifiable Information (PII). Secure Flight employees will receive job-specific privacy refresher training by the end of the calendar year. As stated earlier, we have dedicated privacy personnel on our staff to help with these efforts. As far as tracking decisions pertaining to PII, efforts are already underway to establish a tracking process and we expect a completion date early next year.

TSA greatly appreciates the work GAO put into these audits and looks forward to enhancing the program through addressing their recommendations.

CONCLUSION

TSA's Secure Flight program is a robust system that allows TSA to make Risk-Based Security decisions that are crucial to the security of our transportation systems. Today, Secure Flight not only identifies high-risk passengers by matching them against the TSDB, but it also uses the information to assign all passengers a risk category: High-risk, low-risk, or unknown-risk. At the same time, TSA has also enhanced Secure Flight's privacy oversight mechanisms to protect personally identifiable information.

Secure Flight continues to be the Nation's front-line defense against terrorism targeting the Nation's civil aviation system. It is an incredibly effective tool in identifying individuals of concern for denial of boarding, enhanced screening, or expedited screening. TSA will continue to expand on these successes even further as we work toward our goals of enhancing the passenger experience while at the same time keeping bad actors from doing us harm.

Thank you for the opportunity to testify before you today. I look forward to answering your questions.

Mr. HUDSON. Thank you, Mr. Sadler.

The Chairman now recognizes Mr. Piehota to testify.

STATEMENT OF CHRISTOPHER M. PIEHOTA, DIRECTOR, TERRORIST SCREENING CENTER, FEDERAL BUREAU OF INVESTIGATION, U.S. DEPARTMENT OF JUSTICE

Mr. PIEHOTA. Good afternoon, Chairman Hudson, Ranking Member Richmond, and Members of the subcommittee. Thank you for the opportunity to discuss the Terrorist Screening Center and its National security mission.

Since the creation of the Terrorist Screening Center 11 years ago, the center has played a vital role in the fight against terrorism. The Terrorist Screening Center integrates terrorist identity information from the law enforcement, homeland security, and intelligence communities into a single identities database known as the Terrorist Screening Database, or TSDB.

The TSDB populates the various terrorist screening systems used by the Government. Since its inception, the Terrorist Screening Center has remained committed to protecting the American public from terrorist threats, while simultaneously protecting privacy and safeguarding civil liberties.

The TSDB, commonly referred to as the Terrorist Watch List, contains both known or suspected international and domestic terrorist identity information. The procedure for submitting information on individuals for inclusion on the Terrorist Watch List is referred to as the nomination process.

Nominations originate from credible information developed by the law enforcement, homeland security, and intelligence communities. Federal departments and agencies submit nominations from known or suspected international terrorists to the National Counterterrorism Center, or the NCTC, for inclusion in their Terrorist Identity Datamart Environment, or TIDE database. NCTC reviews the TIDE entries and submits them to the TSC if these entries include sufficient biographic or biometric identifiers and are supported with derogatory information that generally meets the reasonable suspicion standard. In a similar fashion, the FBI collects, stores, and forwards information relating purely to domestic terrorists to the Terrorist Screening Center.

The facts and circumstances pertaining to a nomination should indicate that an individual is known or suspected to be or has been engaged in conduct constituting, in preparation for, in aid of, or related to terrorism or terrorist activities. The reasonable suspicion standard is based upon the totality of circumstances to account for the sometimes fragmentary nature of terrorist information. Mere guesses or hunches are not sufficient to constitute reasonable suspicion.

In addition, nominations cannot be solely based on race, ethnicity, National origin, religious affiliation, or First Amendment-protected activity. Moreover, if the information is to the No-Fly or Selectee lists, the nomination must meet additional screening criteria.

The utility of the watchlisting process is highest when the information is efficiently disseminated to those law enforcement agencies that need it to perform their law enforcement, homeland security, or intelligence missions. As such, the Terrorist Screening Center places a premium on the timely dissemination of terrorist identity data to our screening partners, and the TSC supports the TSA and other partners by providing the No-Fly and Selectee lists for aviation security screening through real-time transactional information transfer.

Throughout the entire watchlisting and screening process, the TSC continues to play a significant role in ensuring that civil liberties are safeguarded and privacy is protected. The goal of the redress process is to provide a timely and fair review of redress inquiries referred to DHS and, when applicable, the Terrorist Screening Center. Individuals who believe they were inconvenienced as a result of screening can submit a redress inquiry through DHS, the Traveler Redress Inquiry Program. We support DHS TRIP by resolving inquiries that appear to be related to terrorist data included in the TSDB.

Upon receipt of a DHS TRIP referral, the Terrorist Screening Center redress program reviews the available information, including information provided by the inquiring party, and determines whether the inquiring party is an exact match to an identity in the TSDB and, if so, whether the identity should continue to be watchlisted in the TSDB or whether the inquiring party's status should be adjusted. As part of the review process, the TSC's redress program coordinates with the agency who had nominated the individual to the Terrorist Watch List and, if warranted, updates the applicable data.

In conclusion, the TSC has firmly established itself as a primary element in the U.S. Government's counterterrorism detection, early warning, and prevention network. As a premier counterterrorism function, the TSC supports its interagency partners in preserving the safety, security, and prosperity of our communities.

Thank you again for the opportunity to discuss the TSC and its National security mission. I look forward to any questions you may have.

[The prepared statement of Mr. Piehota follows:]

PREPARED STATEMENT OF CHRISTOPHER M. PIEHOTA

SEPTEMBER 18, 2014

Good afternoon Chairman Hudson, Ranking Member Richmond and Members of the subcommittee. Thank you for the opportunity to discuss the Terrorist Screening Center (TSC) and its role in the interagency watchlisting and screening process.

Over the past 11 years, the TSC has played a vital role in the fight against terrorism by integrating terrorist identity information from the law enforcement, homeland security, and intelligence communities into a single identities database known as the Terrorist Screening Database (TSDB), which populates the various terrorist screening systems used by the U.S. Government. Throughout this process, the TSC has remained committed to protecting the American public from terrorist threats while simultaneously protecting privacy and safeguarding civil liberties. As our efforts continue to evolve in response to new threats and intelligence, your support provides us with the tools necessary to continue our mission.

TERRORIST NOMINATION PROCESS

The TSDB, commonly referred to as the Terrorist Watch List, contains both international and domestic terrorist identity information. The procedure for submitting information on individuals for inclusion on the Terrorist Watch List is referred to as the nomination process. The nomination process is the most fundamental and singularly important step in the watchlisting process. It is through this process that individuals are added to the Terrorist Watch List. Nominations originate from credible information developed by our intelligence and law enforcement partners. These intelligence and law enforcement agencies are referred to as Originators in the watchlisting community because it is through their work that nominations are developed. Federal departments and agencies submit nominations of known or suspected international terrorists to the National Counterterrorism Center (NCTC) for inclusion in NCTC's Terrorist Identities Datamart Environment (TIDE) database. NCTC reviews TIDE entries and transmits entries to TSC that include sufficient identifiers and are supported with information that meet the reasonable suspicion watchlisting standard described below. Similarly, the FBI collects, stores, and forwards information to the TSC relating to domestic terrorists that may have connections to international terrorism.

Before placing any information into the TSDB, the TSC utilizes a multi-level review process to ensure that the nomination meets the criteria for inclusion. Generally, nominations to the TSDB must satisfy two requirements. First, the facts and circumstances pertaining to the nomination must meet the reasonable suspicion standard of review. Second, the biographic information associated with a nomination must contain sufficient identifying data so that a person being screened can be matched to or disassociated from another watchlisted individual.

Reasonable suspicion requires articulable facts which, taken together with rational inferences, reasonably warrant the determination that an individual "is known or suspected to be or has been engaged in conduct constituting, in preparation for, in aid of or related to terrorism and terrorist activities." The reasonable suspicion standard is based on the totality of the circumstances in order to account for the sometimes fragmentary nature of terrorist information. Due weight must be given to the reasonable inferences that a person can draw from the available facts. Mere guesses or inarticulate "hunches" are not enough to constitute reasonable suspicion. In addition, nominations must not be solely based on race, ethnicity, national origin, religious affiliation, or First Amendment-protected activity, such as free speech, the exercise of religion, freedom of the press, freedom of peaceful assembly, and petitioning the Government for redress of grievances. There are limited exceptions to the reasonable suspicion requirement, which exist to support immigration and border screening by the Department of State and Department of Homeland Security.

Upon receiving the nomination, TSC personnel review the supporting information to assess sufficiency, including accuracy and timeliness. In particular, TSC personnel must make two determinations. First, they evaluate whether the nomination meets the reasonable suspicion standard for inclusion in the TSDB. This includes determining whether the derogatory information provided with the nomination meets the additional requirements for placing an individual on the No-Fly or Selectee list. If a nomination involves a request that an individual be placed on the No-Fly or Selectee list, the nomination must meet additional substantive criteria, above and beyond the "reasonable suspicion" requirement for TSDB nominations. Second, they consider whether the biographic information associated with a nomination contains sufficient identifying data so that a person being screened can be matched to or distinguished from a watchlisted individual on the TSDB.

Upon conclusion of the TSC's review, TSC will either accept or reject the TSDB nomination. If a nomination is accepted, the TSC will create a TSDB record which includes only the "terrorist identifiers" (e.g., name, date of birth, etc.).

Because it is a Sensitive but Unclassified system, the TSDB does not include substantive derogatory information or Classified National security information. This facilitates the sharing of TSDB identifying information with Government screening and law enforcement officers, such as U.S. Customs and Border Protection Officers at ports of entry and State and local law enforcement officers throughout the United States. In addition, TSC personnel are trained on what information is proper to disclose when responding to an inquiry by a Government screening or law enforcement officer, based on the circumstances of the inquiry.

To uphold the directive in Homeland Security Presidential Directive 6 to maintain "thorough, accurate, and current" information, and to protect civil rights and civil liberties, within the TSDB, several quality control measures are continuously applied by nominating agencies, the NCTC, and TSC. These measures include periodic reviews of nominations and TSDB records, including by attorneys, as well as audits of supporting systems to promote the integrity of the information relied upon for maintenance of TSDB records. Nominating agencies have an on-going responsibility to notify NCTC and TSC of any changes that could affect the validity or reliability of TSDB information. In those cases where modification or deletion of a record relating to international terrorism is required, the nominating agency must notify NCTC, which will process the request and transmit it to the TSC for action. For nominations relating to domestic terrorism, the FBI must follow applicable FBI procedures to request that a FBI-nominated TSDB record be modified or deleted.

EXPORT TO SUPPORTED SYSTEMS

Once a known or suspected terrorist is identified and included in the TSDB, TSC ensures the timely dissemination of the terrorist identity data to our screening partners using encrypted electronic exports. The utility of the watchlisting process is highest when the information is efficiently disseminated to those who need it. The TSC uses subject-matter experts, who are experienced analysts and designated agency representatives, to support the U.S. Government watchlisting and screening mission and the screening systems supported by the TSDB. The six major U.S. Government systems supported by the TSDB are: Department of State's Consular Lookout and Support System (CLASS) for passport and visa screening; Department of Homeland Security's (DHS) TECS system for border and port of entry screening; DHS Secure Flight system for air passenger screening (such as against the No-Fly and Selectee lists) by the Transportation Security Administration (TSA); DHS Transportation Vetting System for credentialing transportation and critical infrastructure workers; the Department of Defense for base access and screening; and, the FBI's National Crime and Information Center's Known or Suspected Terrorist File (formerly known as the Violent Gang/Terrorist Organization File (VGTOF)) for domestic law enforcement screening. The TSDB data exported to each of these systems is specifically tailored to the mission, legal authorities, and information technology requirements of the department or agency that maintains the system. Accordingly, each system receives a different subset of data from TSDB. In addition, TSC inserts provisions into its information-sharing agreements requiring its information-sharing partners to properly protect TSDB-derived information, grant access to or release that information only pursuant to the agreement, and to provide appropriate training to individuals granted access to this information.

REDRESS

Throughout the entire watchlisting and screening process the TSC plays a significant role in ensuring that civil liberties are safeguarded and privacy is protected. The TSC led the interagency initiative to develop an effective interagency redress process and maintains a separate unit dedicated to resolving redress matters regarding individuals who believe they have been incorrectly watchlisted. The goal of the redress process is to provide a timely and fair review of redress inquiries referred to the TSC. Working closely with our interagency partners, TSC developed an interagency Memorandum of Understanding (MOU) on Terrorist Watchlist Redress Procedures that was signed in September 2007. The MOU standardizes interagency watch list redress procedures and provides complainants with an opportunity to receive a timely, fair, and accurate review of their redress concerns.

For example, travelers who are denied or delayed boarding or entry into the United States can submit a redress inquiry through the DHS Traveler Redress Inquiry Program, commonly referred to as DHS TRIP. DHS TRIP provides the public with a single point of contact for individuals who have inquiries or seek resolution regarding difficulties they experienced during travel screening at transportation hubs (such as airports and train stations) or during their inspection at a U.S. port of entry. The TSC supports DHS TRIP by helping to resolve complaints that appear to be related to data in the TSDB.

When a traveler's inquiry appears to concern data in the TSDB, DHS TRIP refers the case to the TSC Redress Unit for research into the matter. Upon receipt of a DHS TRIP inquiry, TSC Redress Unit reviews the available information, including the information and documentation provided by the traveler, and determines: (1) Whether the traveler is an exact match to an identity in the TSDB; and, if an exact match exists, (2) whether the identity should continue to be in the TSDB or whether the status should be changed (for example, downgrade a No-Fly record).

If the redress inquiry is a match to an identity in the TSDB, the TSC Redress Unit researches the record and underlying derogatory information, coordinates with the agency that nominated the complainant to the Terrorist Watch List to ensure the information is current and reliable, and, if warranted, updates incorrect or outdated Terrorist Watch List data that may cause the individual difficulty during a screening process. Upon the conclusion of TSC's review, the TSC Redress Unit advises DHS TRIP representatives of the outcome so they can directly respond to the complainant. In some cases, the TSC determines that the individual should remain watchlisted, but may also modify the individual's watch list status accordingly.

In addition, when the TSC is advised through press or Congressional inquiries about individuals who have encountered travel difficulties due to their perceived watch list status, the TSC Redress Unit reviews the pertinent watch list encounter records. If the person is found to be misidentified, the TSC examines our records to determine if there is any additional information that could be used to reduce future misidentifications. At the conclusion of the process, the inquiring entity is notified that all reasonable measures to reduce any future misidentifications have been taken.

Finally, as you may know, there are currently a number of pending court cases involving challenges to administration of the No-Fly List by plaintiffs who allege they have been wrongly denied boarding on an aircraft. We are currently working with our interagency partners on potential changes to the [existing No-Fly List] redress process to ensure that our procedures continue to safeguard civil liberties and privacy. These changes will be made in coordination with other agencies involved in aviation security screening, informed by legal and policy concerns that affect the U.S. Government's administration of the No-Fly List and the overarching redress process. In so doing, the U.S. Government will endeavor to increase transparency for certain individuals denied boarding who believe they are on the No-Fly List and have submitted DHS TRIP inquiries, consistent with the protection of National security and National security information, as well as transportation security.

CONCLUSION

The TSC has a standing commitment to protect the United States and its international partners from terrorist threats while protecting privacy and safeguarding civil liberties. Terrorist watchlisting has been a vital early warning and interdiction tool in the counterterrorism efforts of the United States Government and will continue to serve in this capacity in the future.

Mr. HUDSON. Thank you, Mr. Piehota.

The Chairman now recognizes Ms. Grover to testify.

STATEMENT OF JENNIFER A. GROVER, ACTING DIRECTOR, HOMELAND SECURITY AND JUSTICE, U.S. GOVERNMENT ACCOUNTABILITY OFFICE

Ms. GROVER. Good afternoon, Chairman Hudson, Ranking Member Richmond, and other Members and staff. I am pleased to be here today to discuss TSA's implementation and oversight of the Secure Flight program.

In my remarks, I would like to highlight four points from the reports GAO issued today on Secure Flight. First, what TSA knows about Secure Flight system-matching errors. Second, what TSA knows about screening errors at the checkpoint. Third, initiatives to reduce processing time of passenger requests for redress. Fourth, opportunities to strengthen Secure Flight privacy protections.

First, Secure Flight system-matching errors, which are instances when the Secure Flight system fails to identify a passenger with a reservation on an upcoming flight as being included on a watch list and who therefore should receive additional screening or not be permitted to fly. We found that TSA is lacking key information about how well Secure Flight is achieving its goals, including the extent to which the system misses passengers on the watch lists. We therefore recommend that TSA develop additional performance measures to monitor this and other aspects of the Secure Flight program.

Even without performance measures related to system-matching errors, sometimes TSA becomes aware of such errors through other means. In these cases, the TSA Match Review Board studies the incident to determine what actions are necessary to prevent similar errors. However, TSA has not maintained readily available, accurate information on the number or causes of system-matching errors which would provide a more robust basis for program oversight. Therefore, we also recommend that TSA develop a mechanism to systematically document the number and causes of Secure Flight system-matching errors.

Second, screening errors at the checkpoint, which are instances in which screening personnel have made errors in implementing Secure Flight determinations. We reviewed TSA data from May 2012 through February 2014 and found that such errors have occurred. At some airports TSA officials conduct after-action reviews to identify and address the root causes of these errors. Conducting such reviews across all airports would allow TSA to identify trends and target Nation-wide efforts to address them. We recommend that TSA develop a process to evaluate the root causes of screening errors at all airport checkpoints and implement corrective measures as necessary.

Third, passenger requests for redress, which gives passengers who believe they have been erroneously matched to a watch list an opportunity to address this and prevent it from happening in the future. DHS TRIP, the office that administers the redress process, and the Terrorist Screening Center, which maintains watch lists derived from the Terrorist Screening Database, are taking steps to reduce the processing time for redress applications. In fact, TRIP reduced the redress processing time from an average of 100 to 42 days during fiscal year 2014.

In contrast, the average processing time for redress appeals is significantly longer: 276 days, or about 9 months. This time period is inconsistent with the letter that appeals applicants receive stating that DHS will provide a final agency decision within 60 days. TRIP and TSC have taken steps to reduce the appeals review time, but it will be important for TRIP to monitor progress in this area and consider changes to the 60-day time frame referenced in the appeals letter if necessary.

Fourth, Secure Flight privacy protections to safeguard passengers' personally identifiable information. Let me acknowledge that TSA already has privacy mechanisms in place, including 24/7 audit logs of the Secure Flight system and user events, privacy training for all new Secure Flight staff, and mechanisms to document some privacy-related issues, such as the destruction of passenger data. However, TSA's protections could be further strengthened with the development of annual job-specific privacy training for all Secure Flight employees and through comprehensive documentation of key privacy issues and decisions.

As Mr. Sadler noted, DHS has concurred with all of our recommendations regarding improvements to Secure Flight and is planning for implementation.

Chairman Hudson, Ranking Member Richmond, thank you for the opportunity to testify this afternoon.

[The prepared statement of Ms. Grover follows:]

PREPARED STATEMENT OF JENNIFER A. GROVER

SEPTEMBER 18, 2014

Chairman Hudson, Ranking Member Richmond, and Members of the subcommittee: I am pleased to be here today to discuss the findings from our two September 2014 reports, being released today, in which we assessed the performance of the Department of Homeland Security (DHS) Transportation Security Administration's (TSA) Secure Flight program and related privacy issues.[1] Secure Flight screens approximately 2 million passengers each day, matching passenger information against Federal Government watch lists and other information to assign each passenger a risk category. By identifying those passengers who may pose security risks, Secure Flight helps protect against potential acts of terrorism that might target the Nation's civil aviation system.

In response to requirements of the Intelligence Reform and Terrorism Prevention Act of 2004, and a recommendation of the National Commission on Terrorist Attacks upon the United States (the 9/11 Commission), TSA developed and implemented Secure Flight in order to assume from air carriers the function of matching passengers against watch lists maintained by the Federal Government.[2] At the time, TSA matched passengers against two watch lists, which were intended to identify high-risk individuals: (1) The No-Fly List, composed of individuals who should be precluded from boarding an aircraft, and (2) the Selectee List, composed of individuals who should receive enhanced screening at the airport security checkpoint. The No-Fly and Selectee Lists are subsets of the Terrorist Screening Database (TSDB)—the U.S. Government's consolidated watch list of known or suspected terrorists maintained by the Terrorist Screening Center (TSC), a multi-agency organization administered by the Federal Bureau of Investigation.

After initiating development of Secure Flight in August 2004, TSA began implementing it in 2009, and completed transitioning foreign and domestic air carriers to the program in November 2010.[3] Secure Flight now screens passengers and certain nontraveling individuals on all domestic and international commercial flights to, from, and within the United States; certain flights overflying the continental United States; and international point-to-point flights operated by U.S. aircraft operators.[4]

Secure Flight can have inadvertent and potentially inappropriate impacts on the traveling public, such as when passengers are identified as high-risk because they share a similar name and date of birth with an individual listed on a watch list, and thus experience delays and inconveniences during their travels. DHS's Traveler Redress Inquiry Program (DHS TRIP) provides passengers who have been denied boarding, or identified for additional screening, with an opportunity to be cleared if they are determined not to be a match to TSDB-based watch list records (i.e., misidentified) or if they have been wrongly identified as the subject of a TSDB watch list record (i.e., mislisted).[5]

My testimony today highlights the key findings of our two reports on Secure Flight.[6] My statement will address the extent to which: (1) TSA's performance measures appropriately assess progress toward achieving the Secure Flight program goals, (2) TSA ensures that Secure Flight screening determinations for passengers are fully implemented at airport security checkpoints, (3) DHS's redress process addresses the delays and inconveniences that result from Secure Flight screening, and

---

[1] GAO, *Secure Flight: TSA Should Take Additional Steps to Determine Program Effectiveness*, GAO–14–531 (Washington, DC: Sept. 9, 2014), and *Secure Flight: TSA Could Take Additional Steps to Strengthen Privacy Oversight Mechanisms*, GAO–14–647 (Washington, DC: Sept. 9, 2014).

[2] See Pub. L. No. 108–458, § 4012(a), 118 Stat. 3638, 3714–18 (2004) (codified at 49 U.S.C. § 44903(j)(2)(C)). The 9/11 Commission, *The 9/11 Commission Report: Final Report of the National Commission on Terrorist Attacks upon the United States*, July 2004. TSA efforts to develop a computer-assisted passenger prescreening system predated the Intelligence Reform and Terrorism Prevention Act and the report of the 9/11 Commission.

[3] TSA began implementing Secure Flight pursuant to the Secure Flight Program Final Rule, issued in October 2008. See 73 Fed. Reg. 64,018 (Oct. 28, 2008).

[4] Secure Flight screens certain nontraveling individuals, such as escorts for minor, elderly, and disabled passengers, who are authorized to access the airport's sterile area—the portion of an airport defined in the airport security program that provides passengers access to boarding aircraft and to which access is generally controlled through the screening of persons and property. See 49 C.F.R. § 1540.5. For purposes of this report, the term "commercial flight" encompasses all U.S. and foreign air carrier operations covered by and subject to the Secure Flight Final Rule. See 49 C.F.R. § 1560.3 (defining "covered flight" for purposes of the Secure Flight Program).

[5] DHS established DHS TRIP in February 2007 as the central processing point within DHS for travel-related redress inquiries. See 49 U.S.C. § 44903(j)(2)(G)(i) (requiring the establishment of a timely and fair process for individuals identified as a threat as a result of TSA's passenger prescreening system to appeal the determination and correct any erroneous information).

[6] GAO–14–531 addressed the operations of the Secure Flight program, including TSA's implementation of screening determinations at the checkpoint and performance measures for the Secure Flight program. GAO–14–647 addressed Secure Flight's privacy oversight mechanisms and DHS's redress process.

(4) TSA has implemented privacy oversight mechanisms to address Secure Flight privacy requirements.

For the September 2014 reports, we analyzed documentation of TSA's program goals and performance measures for fiscal years 2011 through 2013 and assessed these measures against provisions of the Government Performance and Results Act (GPRA).[7] We also analyzed a list that TSA compiled at our request of missed passengers on two high-risk lists (including the reasons for these matching errors) that occurred from November 2010 through July 2013. We analyzed certain TSA data on screener performance at airport security checkpoints from May 2012, when TSA began tracking these data, through February 2014, when we conducted the analysis. We also reviewed relevant DHS TRIP redress and appeals data for fiscal years 2011 through 2013. In addition, to evaluate TSA's documentation of Secure Flight privacy issues and decisions and TSA's privacy training for Secure Flight staff, we reviewed relevant documents prepared by TSA privacy officials and contract staff, including privacy compliance validation reports for the period from April 2012 through April 2013, monthly status reports prepared by TSA's privacy contractor for the period from March 2013 through April 2014, and privacy training documents. We interviewed TSA and other DHS officials who are responsible for aspects of Secure Flight and DHS TRIP, as well as TSA officials at nine airports, which we selected based on a variety of factors, such as volume of passengers screened and geographic dispersion. Our September 2014 reports provide further details on our scope and methodology.[8] The work upon which this statement is based was conducted in accordance with generally accepted Government auditing standards.

BACKGROUND

Since its implementation in 2009, Secure Flight has changed from a program that identifies passengers as high-risk solely by matching them against the No-Fly and Selectee Lists to one that assigns passengers a risk category: High-risk, low-risk, or unknown-risk. In 2010, following the December 2009 attempted attack on a U.S.-bound flight, which exposed gaps in how agencies used watch lists to screen individuals, TSA began using risk-based criteria to identify additional high-risk passengers who may not be in the TSDB, but who should be subject to enhanced screening procedures. Further, in 2011, TSA began screening passengers against additional identities in the TSDB that are not already included on the No-Fly or Selectee Lists. In addition, as part of TSA PreCheck™, a 2011 program through which TSA designates passengers as low-risk for expedited screening, TSA began screening against several new lists of preapproved low-risk travelers. TSA also began conducting TSA PreCheck™ risk assessments, an activity distinct from matching against lists that uses the Secure Flight system to assign passengers scores based upon their travel-related data, for the purpose of identifying them as low-risk for a specific flight. See appendix I for a list of Secure Flight screening activities.

To conduct Secure Flight screening, TSA uses passenger information, known collectively as Secure Flight Passenger Data (SFPD), which is collected by aircraft operators.[9] Once this screening is conducted, Secure Flight then sends the air carrier a determination of how the passenger will be screened at the checkpoint if provided a boarding pass. These determinations include a "TSA PreCheck™-eligible" message for passengers who may receive expedited screening; a "cleared" message for passengers found not to match any high- or low-risk list and who, therefore, will generally receive standard screening; and a "selectee" message for passengers who should undergo enhanced screening.[10] For passengers matching the No-Fly List, the air carrier is precluded from issuing a boarding pass.

---

[7] Government Performance and Results Act of 1993, Pub. L. No. 103–62, 107 Stat. 285 (1993). GPRA was updated by the GPRA Modernization Act of 2010. Pub. L. No. 111–352, 124 Stat. 3866 (2011).

[8] GAO–14–531 and GAO–14–647.

[9] See 49 C.F.R. § 1560.3. SFPD includes personally identifiable information, such as full name, gender, date of birth, passport information (if available), and certain nonpersonally identifiable information, such as itinerary information and the unique number associated with a travel record (record number locator).

[10] Standard screening typically includes passing through a walk-through metal detector or Advanced Imaging Technology screening, which identifies objects or anomalies on the outside of the body, and X-ray screening for the passenger's accessible property. Enhanced screening includes, in addition to the procedures applied during a typical standard screening experience, a pat-down and an explosive trace detection search or physical search of the interior of the passenger's accessible property, electronics, and footwear. Expedited screening typically includes walk-through metal detector screening and X-ray screening of the passenger's accessible property, but unlike in standard screening, travelers do not have to, among other things, remove

Continued

Passengers who believe they have been unfairly denied boarding or identified for additional screening may apply to DHS TRIP using an on-line application, by e-mail, or by mail. If DHS TRIP determines that an individual is still a potential match to a TSDB watch list record, it refers the matter to TSC for further review. TSC then conducts its own review of whether the individual has been misidentified to a watch list and whether, based on the most current available information and criteria for inclusion on the list, the individual is either correctly assigned to the list or is wrongly assigned and should be removed from the list. If DHS TRIP and TSC determine that no change in the passenger's status is warranted, the passenger is notified of this decision, and depending on the determination, some passengers are permitted the opportunity to appeal the decision. When passengers appeal, DHS TRIP forwards all completed appeals paperwork to TSC. TSC analysts are to review all derogatory information maintained on the appellant to make a written recommendation to TSA on the appeal. TSA then reviews TSC's recommendation through its own internal process, which can include going back to TSC for additional information, before the TSA administrator makes the final determination to uphold the appellant's status, recommend that TSC downgrade the appellant to another TSDB-based list, or recommend that TSC remove the appellant from the list.[11]

TSA LACKS KEY INFORMATION TO DETERMINE WHETHER THE SECURE FLIGHT PROGRAM IS ACHIEVING ITS GOALS

In September 2014, we reported that Secure Flight has established program goals that reflect new program functions since 2009 to identify additional types of high-risk and also low-risk passengers; however, current program performance measures do not allow Secure Flight to fully assess its progress toward achieving all of its goals. For example, to measure performance toward its goals that address the system's ability to accurately identify passengers on various watch lists, Secure Flight collects various types of data, including the number of passengers TSA identifies as matches to high- and low-risk lists. However, we found that Secure Flight does not have measures to assess the extent of system-matching errors—for example, the extent to which Secure Flight is missing passengers who are actual matches to these lists. In addition, we found that Secure Flight's measures do not provide information on progress toward the program's goal to incorporate additional risk-based security capabilities to streamline processes and accommodate additional aviation populations, in part because the goal itself did not specify how performance toward the goal should be measured.

We concluded that additional measures that address key performance aspects related to program goals, and that clearly identify the activities necessary to achieve goals, in accordance with the Government Performance and Results Act, would allow TSA to more fully assess progress toward its goals. For example, a measure that reflects misidentifications to all high-risk lists could help TSA appropriately gauge its performance with respect to its goal of limiting such misidentifications. Likewise, establishing measures that clearly represent the performance necessary to achieve the program's goal that addresses risk-based security capabilities will allow Secure Flight to determine the extent to which it is meeting its goal of adapting the Secure Flight system for different risk-based screening activities. Without measures that provide a more complete understanding of Secure Flight's performance, TSA cannot compare actual with desired results to understand how well the system is achieving these goals. Therefore, we recommended in September 2014 that TSA develop additional measures to address key performance aspects related to each program goal, and ensure these measures clearly identify the activities necessary to achieve progress toward the goal. DHS concurred with our recommendation and stated that TSA's Office of Intelligence and Analysis (OIA) will evaluate its current Secure Flight performance goals and measures and develop new performance measures as necessary.

We also found in September 2014 that TSA lacks timely and reliable information on all known cases of Secure Flight system matching errors. TSA officials told us at the time of our review that when TSA receives information related to matching errors of the Secure Flight system, the Secure Flight Match Review Board reviews this information to determine if any actions could be taken to prevent similar errors

---

their belts, shoes, or light outerwear. The Secure Flight system may also return an error response to air carriers regarding passengers for whom Secure Flight has received incomplete data.

[11] TSC, in the course of its review, may also find the appellant was misidentified to a TSDB-based list.

from happening again.[12] We identified instances in which the Match Review Board discussed system-matching errors, investigated possible actions to address these errors, and implemented changes to strengthen system performance. However, we also found that TSA does not have readily-available or complete information on the extent and causes of system-matching errors. We recommended that TSA develop a mechanism to systematically document the number and causes of the Secure Flight system's matching errors, in accordance with Federal internal control standards. Such a mechanism would provide Secure Flight more timely and reliable information on the extent to which the system is performing as intended. DHS concurred with our recommendation and stated that TSA's OIA will develop a more robust process to track all known cases in which the Secure Flight system has made a matching error, and that the Secure Flight Match Review Board will conduct reviews to identify potential system improvement measures on a quarterly basis.

TSA HAS PROCESSES IN PLACE TO IMPLEMENT SECURE FLIGHT SCREENING DETERMINATIONS AT CHECKPOINTS, BUT COULD TAKE FURTHER ACTION TO ADDRESS SCREENING ERRORS

In September 2014, we reported that TSA has processes in place to implement Secure Flight screening determinations at airport checkpoints, but could take steps to enhance these processes. Screening personnel at airport checkpoints are primarily responsible for ensuring that passengers receive a level of screening that corresponds to the level of risk determined by Secure Flight by verifying passengers' identities and identifying passengers' screening designations. TSA information from May 2012 through February 2014 that we assessed indicates that screening personnel have made errors in implementing Secure Flight determinations at the checkpoint. TSA officials we spoke with at five of the nine airports where we conducted interviews conduct after-action reviews of screening errors at the checkpoint and have used these reviews to take action to address the root causes of those errors. However, we found that TSA does not have a systematic process for evaluating the root causes of these screening errors at the checkpoint across airports, which could allow TSA to identify trends across airports and target Nation-wide efforts to address these issues.

Officials with TSA's Office of Security Operations (OSO) told us in the course of our September 2014 review that evaluating the root causes of screening errors would be helpful and stated they were in the early stages of forming a group to discuss these errors. However, TSA was not able to provide documentation of the group's membership, purpose, goals, time frames, or methodology. *Standards for Internal Control in the Federal Government* states that managers should compare actual performance with expected results and analyze significant differences.[13] Therefore, we recommended in September 2014 that TSA develop a process for evaluating the root causes of screening errors at the checkpoint and then implement corrective measures to address those causes. DHS concurred with our recommendation and stated that TSA's OSO will collect and evaluate data on screening errors to identify root causes and work to implement corrective measures. Uncovering and addressing the root causes of screening errors could allow TSA to strengthen security screening at airports by reducing the number of these errors at the checkpoint.

DHS TRIP ADDRESSES INCONVENIENCES AND DELAYS RELATED TO TSDB-BASED LISTS, AND IS TAKING ACTIONS TO REDUCE CASE-PROCESSING TIME

In September 2014, we reported that DHS TRIP affords passengers adversely affected by TSA screening processes an opportunity to address inconveniences and delays associated with being potentially misidentified to a TSDB-based list.[14] Passengers who are determined to have been incorrectly matched to or listed on high-risk lists based on the TSDB are added to a list of passengers known as the TSA Cleared List, which allows them to be cleared (not identified as high-risk) nearly

---

[12] Secure Flight's Match Review Board—a multi-departmental entity—and associated Match Review Working Group review performance measurement results and recommend changes to improve system performance, among other things.

[13] GAO, *Internal Control: Standards for Internal Control in the Federal Government*, GAO/AIMD–00–21.3.1. (Washington, DC: Nov. 1, 1999).

[14] The specific impacts experienced by a passenger who has been matched to a watch list vary depending upon the list to which the passenger is matched. For example, an individual with a name similar to that of someone who is on the No-Fly list likely will be unable to utilize the convenience of internet, curbside, and airport kiosk check-in options.

100 percent of the time.[15] The DHS TRIP process also allows passengers determined to have been improperly included on a TSDB-based list (mislisted) to be removed, minimizing the likelihood they will be identified as matches during future travels.[16] Although DHS TRIP is not able to provide redress for passengers who may have been misidentified to high-risk, rules-based lists (TSA's lists of high-risk passengers who, based on risk-based criteria, should be subject to enhanced screening procedures though they may not be in the TSDB), according to TSA officials, TSA procedures for using such lists mitigate impacts on these passengers. These procedures may result in TSA removing passengers from the lists, which ensures that passengers who are misidentified to those individuals will no longer be identified as a match, and thus delayed or inconvenienced as a result.

We also found that DHS has reduced its average processing time for redress cases and is taking actions to further reduce processing times. Specifically, we found that DHS TRIP officials took several steps in fiscal year 2013 to reduce the overall processing time and a backlog of redress cases including, for example, automating its response to DHS TRIP applicants and hiring additional staff. According to DHS TRIP officials, at the beginning of fiscal year 2014, DHS TRIP's average case-processing time for redress cases was approximately 100 days, and as of June 2014, the average case-processing time was about 42 days. In January 2014, DHS TRIP also reduced its target for one of its key performance indicators—average number of days for DHS TRIP redress cases to be closed—from 93 to 78 days.

In addition, we reported in September 2014 that DHS TRIP is taking actions to reduce processing times for appeals cases. Appeals applicants receive a letter stating that DHS will provide a final agency decision on the appeal within 60 days of receipt of the appeal. However, we found that the average total processing time for the appeals process for fiscal years 2011 through 2013 was 276 days. In fiscal year 2013, DHS TRIP began taking several actions to make the appeals process more structured and reduce the overall review time, including, among other things, developing and distributing documents that provide information on the status and outcome of each appeal case and implementing a more formalized process for reviewing appeals. In January 2014, DHS TRIP also established intermediate and long-term performance goals for the appeals process for the first time. Specifically, the intermediate performance goal calls for an average total processing time of 92 days, while the long-term performance goal calls for an average processing time of 60 days, consistent with the time frame DHS TRIP commits to achieving in the letter informing applicants of their right to appeal. According to DHS TRIP officials, the agency plans to periodically assess its progress toward achieving its intermediate and long-term goals for reducing appeals-processing times. Officials stated that if DHS TRIP finds it is not making adequate progress by February 2015—about 1 year after the program began taking specific actions to reduce the overall review

---

[15] Upon receipt of a complete application, DHS TRIP sends a notification of receipt with a redress control number to the passenger. DHS TRIP adds the name, date of birth, and redress control number of applicants determined not to match a TSDB-based list to the TSA Cleared List. Passengers included on the TSA Cleared List must then submit their redress control number when making a reservation to allow the Secure Flight system to recognize and clear them. Because of the application of other TSA security measures, such as random selection, an individual's presence on the Cleared List may diminish, but will not preclude, the possibility of being selected for enhanced screening.

[16] During the pendency of this review, various courts have issued decisions relating to the No-Fly List and DHS TRIP. For example, in January 2014, a judge of the U.S. District Court for the Northern District of California issued a findings of fact, conclusions of law, and order for relief in the case of *Ibrahim* v. *Dep't of Homeland Security*, No. C 06–00545 WHA (N.D. Cal. Jan 14, 2014) (redacted). Specifically, the court found that in this matter, which involved facts dating back to 2004, the plaintiff had been placed on the No-Fly List as a result of a Federal Bureau of Investigation agent's human error and that, among other things, the redress response letter provided to the plaintiff by the redress program in place prior to the establishment of DHS TRIP was inadequate at the time because the response was vague and "fell short of providing any assurance to [the Plaintiff] . . . that the mistake had been traced down in all its forms and venues and corrected." In June 2014, a judge of the U.S. District Court for the District of Oregon issued an opinion and order concluding, among other things, that because DHS TRIP procedures do not afford individuals the requirements of due process in so much as they do not provide them with notice regarding their status on the No-Fly List and the reasons for placement on the list, "the absence of any meaningful procedures to afford Plaintiffs the opportunity to contest their placement on the No-Fly List violates Plaintiffs' rights to procedural due process." See *Latif* v. *Holder*, No. 3:10–cv–00750–BR (D. Or. June 24, 2014). According to a Joint Supplemental Status Report filed with the district court on September 3, 2014, the Government is in the process of developing revised procedures and is committed to complete this and other steps and issue final orders prior to February 2, 2015. Our review focused on the procedures and data relating to implementation of the DHS TRIP redress and appeals processes and did not evaluate DHS TRIP on sufficiency of procedural due process grounds.

time—it would first evaluate whether further changes and improvements could be made to shorten the appeals process before considering, in collaboration with TSC and the DHS Screening Coordination Office, a change to the 60-day time frame stated in the appeals letter.

TSA HAS IMPLEMENTED OVERSIGHT MECHANISMS TO ADDRESS PASSENGER PRIVACY REQUIREMENTS, BUT ADDITIONAL ACTIONS COULD BETTER ENSURE FULL COMPLIANCE

TSA has taken steps to implement privacy oversight mechanisms, but, as we reported in September 2014, additional actions could allow TSA to sustain and strengthen its efforts. Overall, TSA has implemented mechanisms to identify privacy implications associated with program operations and address them as necessary. For example, TSA has regularly-updated privacy documents to address changes in the Secure Flight program and maintains and reviews audit logs of Secure Flight system and user events, such as requests to access the system that generates reports on Secure Flight activities. TSA has also implemented privacy training for new Secure Flight staff, and all DHS employees receive annual privacy training. However, we found that existing Secure Flight staff do not receive job-specific privacy refresher training consistent with Office of Management and Budget (OMB) requirements.[17] For example, TSA updated its privacy training for new Secure Flight staff in December 2013 to reflect new privacy risks unique to Secure Flight's expanded screening activities. However, because the DHS privacy refresher training for existing staff is not job-specific, staff who joined Secure Flight prior to December 2013 may not have received privacy training specific to these new screening activities. We recommended that TSA provide at least annual job-specific privacy refresher training in order to further strengthen Secure Flight's protection of personally identifiable information. DHS concurred with our recommendation and stated that TSA's OIA will develop and deliver job-specific privacy refresher training for all Secure Flight staff.

We also reported in September 2014 that TSA documents some aspects of its Secure Flight privacy oversight mechanisms, such as scheduled destructions of passenger data and reviews of planned changes to the Secure Flight system. However, TSA does not have a mechanism to comprehensively document and track key privacy-related issues and decisions that arise through the development and use of Secure Flight—a mechanism TSA planned to develop when Secure Flight implementation began in 2009. In the course of our September 2014 review, TSA's Secure Flight privacy officer told us that, in the absence of such a system, Secure Flight relies on its privacy contract staff to oversee and monitor privacy protections, in consultation with the designated Secure Flight program privacy officer and the TSA Privacy Officer. However, it is unknown whether this ad hoc communication would be sustained after a personnel change in Secure Flight's privacy team or contractor personnel, and whether privacy-related decisions previously made would continue to be implemented without documentation to inform new staff. Therefore, to help TSA ensure that these decisions are carried into the future in the event of a change in personnel, we recommended that TSA comprehensively document and track key privacy-related issues and decisions, in accordance with Federal internal control standards. DHS concurred with our recommendation and stated that it will develop a mechanism to document such issues and decisions.

Chairman Hudson, Ranking Member Richmond, and Members of the subcommittee, this concludes my prepared testimony. I look forward to answering any questions that you may have.

---

[17] See Office of Management and Budget, *Safeguarding Against and Responding to the Breach of Personally Identifiable Information*, OMB Memorandum M–07–16 (Washington, DC: 2007).

APPENDIX I.—SECURE FLIGHT SCREENING ACTIVITIES

Screening Activity	Description
No-Fly List (high-risk)	The No-Fly List is a subset of the Terrorist Screening Database (TSDB), the U.S. Government's consolidated watch list of known or suspected terrorists maintained by the Terrorist Screening Center (TSC), a multi-agency organization administered by the Federal Bureau of Investigation. The No-Fly List contains records of individuals who are suspected of posing or known to pose a threat to aviation or National security and are prohibited from boarding an aircraft or entering the sterile area of an airport. Secure Flight has matched passengers against the No-Fly List since 2009.
Selectee List (high-risk)	The Selectee List is a subset of the TSDB containing records of individuals who must undergo enhanced security screening before being permitted to enter the sterile area or board an aircraft. Secure Flight has matched against the Selectee List since 2009.
Expanded Selectee List (high-risk).	The Expanded Selectee List includes terrorist records in the TSDB with a complete name and date of birth that meet the reasonable suspicion standard to be considered a known or suspected terrorist, but that do not meet the criteria to be placed on the No-Fly or Selectee Lists [1] Secure Flight began matching against the Expanded Selectee List in April 2011.
Transportation Security Administration (TSA) rules-based lists (high-risk).	The high-risk rules-based lists include two lists of passengers who may not be known or suspected terrorists, but who, according to intelligence-driven, scenario-based rules developed by TSA in consultation with U.S. Customs and Border Protection (CBP), may pose an increased risk to transportation or National security.
Centers for Disease Control and Prevention (CDC) Do Not Board List (high-risk).	The CDC Do Not Board List is managed by CDC. It includes individuals who pose a significant health risk to other travelers and are not allowed to fly.
TSA PreCheck™ lists (low-risk).	TSA PreCheck™ lists include lists of pre-approved, low-risk travelers, such as certain members of CBP's Trusted Traveler programs, members of the U.S. armed forces, Congressional Medal of Honor Society members, and Members of Congress—groups of individuals TSA has determined pose a low risk to transportation or National security—as well as a PreCheck™ list created by TSA and composed of individuals who apply and are pre-approved as low-risk travelers through the PreCheck™ Application Program.[2] Secure Flight began matching against its first set of low-risk lists, CBP Trusted Traveler Lists, in October 2011 and instituted the PreCheck™ Application Program in December 2013.
TSA PreCheck™ Disqualification List (ineligible for low-risk).	The PreCheck™ Disqualification List is a list of individuals who, based upon their involvement in violations of security regulations of sufficient severity or frequency (e.g., bringing a loaded firearm to the checkpoint), are disqualified from receiving expedited screening for some period of time or permanently.

Screening Activity	Description
TSA PreCheck™ risk assessments (low-risk).	Secure Flight assesses certain travel-related information submitted by passengers and assigns them scores that correspond to a likelihood of being eligible for expedited screening for a specific flight. Secure Flight began performing these assessments for selected frequent flier members in October 2011 and, in October 2013, began using them to evaluate all passengers not determined to be a match to a high-risk or low-risk list.

Source.—GAO analysis of TSA and TSC information. GAO–14–796T

[1] All TSDB-based watch lists utilized by the Secure Flight program contain records determined to have met TSC's reasonable suspicion standard. In general, to meet the reasonable suspicion standard, the agency nominating an individual for inclusion in the TSDB must consider the totality of information available that, taken together with rational inferences from that information, reasonably warrants a determination that an individual is known or suspected to be or have been knowingly engaged in conduct constituting, in preparation for, in aid of, or related to terrorism or terrorist activities. To be included on the No-Fly and Selectee Lists, individuals must meet criteria specific to these lists. The TSDB, which is the U.S. Government's consolidated watch list of known or suspected terrorists, also contains records on additional populations of individuals that do not meet the reasonable suspicion standard articulated above but that other Federal agencies utilize to support their border and immigration screening missions. In addition, according to TSA officials, Secure Flight does not utilize all terrorist records in the TSDB because records with partial data (i.e., without first name, surname, and date of birth) could result in a significant increase in the number of passengers misidentified.

[2] Individuals on all low-risk lists receive a Known Traveler Number that they must submit when making travel reservations to be identified as low-risk. See 49 C.F.R. § 1560.3 (defining "Known Traveler Number"). TSA also refers to these lists as Known Traveler lists.

Mr. HUDSON. Thank you, Ms. Grover.

We appreciate all of the witnesses for being here, and thank you for your service to our country.

I now recognize myself for 5 minutes to ask questions.

We will start, Mr. Piehota, we know that an increasing number of Westerners, including Americans, have joined the fight in Iraq and Syria. How confident are you in our ability to track these foreign fighters and ensure that they are being added to the terrorist screening database, including the No-Fly List?

Mr. PIEHOTA. The U.S. Government has a very capable watchlisting and screening enterprise, and I have a high amount of confidence in the abilities of my partners to identify and report known or suspected terrorist identities to the Terrorist Screening Center, and I have a high bit of confidence in the Terrorist Screening Center's ability to export that information to be used by our partners in countering the terrorist threat.

Mr. HUDSON. I appreciate that.

Mr. Sadler, do you want to comment on that at all?

Mr. SADLER. Well, I would say that we have a very close working relationship with the Terrorist Screening Center, as we do with all our Federal partners. It is important to understand that when that intelligence comes in, that when it goes into the organizations that will nominate to the Terrorist Screening Center and when the Terrorist Screening Center nominates those individuals to the watch list, we come in and do our job and we operationalize that data.

So I just want to make the point, we have got a great working relationship with all of our partners, and I think we are doing a good job with this.

Mr. HUDSON. Great. Well, it is important that we do.

Mr. Piehota, has the number of individuals on the No-Fly List grown significantly due to the situation in Syria and Iraq?

Mr. PIEHOTA. We can't correlate any significant increase in the TSDB populations due to the overseas activities right now.

Mr. HUDSON. How has the Terrorist Screening Center streamlined the watch list process and improved information sharing within the intelligence community? I mean, you both said that there is a good working relationship there, but could you maybe give us some specifics of how you have made those improvements?

Mr. PIEHOTA. Well, first the Terrorist Screening Center has improved its policy, its protocol, and its technical infrastructure over the past few years to remove manual processes, lower potential for human error, and as well as to send information to our watchlisting and screening partners in a real-time fashion.

As information is processed at the Terrorist Screening Center, seconds later it shows up with our partners so they can do near-real-time screening as well, a significant technical increase in information management.

We have also participated with our partners in various committees, interagency functions, and collaborative projects that have brought our organizations close together, that we have common operating perspectives, and, as Mr. Sadler said, we work exceptionally well together, and I would daresay that our relationship with TSA has never been closer or more effective than it is right now.

Mr. HUDSON. Great.

Mr. Sadler, recently we learned that a former employee at the Minneapolis-St. Paul Airport was killed while fighting for ISIS in Syria. While employed at the airport, this individual held credentials that allowed him to work as a fuel technician and a cleaner with access to sterile areas of the airport as well as the tarmac and the aircraft itself.

Can you explain how TSA works to mitigate the insider threat at airports across the country, especially in light of this latest situation?

Mr. SADLER. Well, every individual that is issued an airport credential is sent into my office, and we vet those individuals on a daily basis against the Terrorist Screening Database. We also do some other checks on them as well. So we are very cognizant of the population that works at the airport.

That is just my piece of it. You also have to understand that we have personnel at the airport. We have great relationships with the FBI, with State and local authorities at those individual airports as well. But my part of it is to take that information and vet it on a daily basis. So if a change comes through from the Terrorist Screening Center we will know very quickly what that change is and what it means to our vetted population.

Mr. HUDSON. Great. I appreciate that.

Ms. Grover, I have become a fan of your work over the years. Appreciate you being here with us again. You talked about some of the difficulties of the checkpoint, and you mentioned in your written statement about fraudulent IDs, people being able to avoid sort of the No-Fly List or the advanced screening.

How is TSA addressing this vulnerability posed by fraudulent IDs and boarding passes?

Ms. GROVER. TSA is making better progress with boarding pass issues than the issue of potential fraudulent IDs, I would say. They have boarding pass scanners in place at many, but not all of the airport checkpoints, and the scanners are designed to provide support to the travel document checker who works there to confirm that the boarding pass is genuine, and then it alerts the travel document checker to the specific level of screening that that individual is supposed to receive.

As far as confirming that the identification that individuals are using is genuine, that is still the responsibility of the travel document checker at this point. TSA has awarded a contract for the development of credential authentication technology, but it was just awarded in April, and I believe it is still in the proof-of-concept stage, so that technology support is still quite a ways out.

Mr. HUDSON. Thank you.

My time has expired and so I will recognize the Ranking Member, Mr. Richmond, for any questions he may have.

Mr. RICHMOND. Thank you, Mr. Chairman.

Mr. Piehota, according to publicly-available data from TSC, as of September 2011 there were approximately 16,000 individuals on the No-Fly List and approximately 16,000 individuals on the Selectee List. What are the current statistics for those numbers of people who are on the No-Fly and Selectee lists?

Mr. PIEHOTA. The Terrorist Screening Center currently stands at about 800,000 identities. For those identities, for the No-Fly List, we are looking at about 8 percent of the overall population of the TSDB are watchlisted at the No-Fly level; about 3 percent of the overall population of the TSDB is watchlisted at the Selectee level.

Mr. RICHMOND. As I play around with that, how many of those individuals on the No-Fly List are U.S. persons?

Mr. PIEHOTA. Approximately 0.8 percent of the overall TSDB population.

Mr. RICHMOND. A lot of times what we deal with, and we develop policies in theory, and in theory they make a lot of sense, and in reality we either didn't go far enough or it just doesn't make sense. As I look at all the people on the No-Fly List, it just does not make common sense to me that you can be on the No-Fly List, where we don't want you flying on our planes, but you can go and enroll in flight school and learn how to fly a plane.

Can you all just give me your assessment of why we would have a policy where you can't fly, but you can go learn how to fly a plane? Am I missing a distinction?

Mr. SADLER. I will take that one, sir. So any foreign applicant who wants to learn how to fly an aircraft gets vetted prior to them receiving training. So whether they are training here, if it is an FAA-certified school, whether they are training here, whether they are training overseas, we vet them.

Any U.S. person gets vetted through the FAA process. So anyone who has an FAA certificate, a student pilot, whatever that happens to be, that comes into my office, we vet those individuals on a daily basis against the TSDB. So they are all vetted.

Mr. RICHMOND. Right. But if we don't want them even flying on a plane, why would we want them to learn how to fly a plane?

Mr. SADLER. If they are on the watch list, No-Fly, they do not learn how to fly a plane. So the foreign applicants get vetted against the No-Fly List and the full TSDB, and they are denied their training application if we determine that they are on that watch list.

Mr. RICHMOND. So everyone on the No-Fly List and the Selectee List, they are barred from flight school?

Mr. SADLER. There are other operational considerations whenever you vet an individual, and I would be happy to talk about that in a closed setting, but they are all vetted through the watch list.

Mr. RICHMOND. Okay. I just want to make sure we are saying the same thing. If they are on the watch list, they can't go to flight school?

Mr. SADLER. It depends on the situation, sir, and that is why I said I would like to talk to you about this in a closed session.

Mr. RICHMOND. Well, thank you.

Did anybody else want to respond to that?

Ms. Grover, GAO noted in its Secure Flight effectiveness report that TSA has asserted that it is difficult to measure the extent to which the Secure Flight system may miss passengers on a high-risk list in real time, but used proxy methods to accomplish this when the system was under development. Should TSA reinstate the use of proxy methods to better assess the rates at which a watchlisted passenger may be missed by the Secure Flight program?

Ms. GROVER. Yes, sir, that is exactly the sort of strategy that would allow TSA to have some additional information about the extent to which the Secure Flight system is accurately identifying all of the individuals that it needs to identify.

When they were first developing the Secure Flight program they used simulated passenger lists and watch lists to be able to approximate the accuracy of the system, and that would be something that they could use on a regular basis to get information about how well the system is working and the likelihood of misses occurring.

They also have a similar system that they use right now when they are considering changes to the way the match process is working that allows them to use historical data, just from the past 7 days, to say, if we make this change, does it improve the matching rate or does it introduce more errors. So any of those approaches would be better than the current situation, which is really no information about the number of misses that are occurring on a regular basis.

Mr. RICHMOND. Thank you.

I see my time has expired, so I yield back.

Mr. HUDSON. Thank the gentleman.

The Chairman now recognizes the gentlelady from Indiana, Mrs. Brooks, for any questions she may have.

Mrs. BROOKS. Thank you, Mr. Chairman, and thank you for calling this hearing on this most important topic.

Mr. Sadler, how does the TSA know that individuals who are on the watch list are not experiencing the expedited screening through TSA's PreCheck, like managed inclusion, which I am seeing more and more? I fly in and out of the Indianapolis Airport, that is a managed inclusion site. How do we know that they are not being chosen and put into managed inclusion?

Mr. SADLER. Well, the first thing, I just want to go back, if you don't mind, ma'am. We do have information on the efficiency and effectiveness of our system. We are looking at new test data, and that new test data is going to be developed based on our experience of vetting 3.7 billion records since we implemented Secure Flight. So we have a pretty good idea of what we are doing. We can improve. We appreciate GAO's recommendations, and we concur with those and we are going to implement those.

So everyone who goes through that airport is going to be prescreened by TSA. So they should have a marking on the boarding pass. That marking should be identified. That should preclude them from going into managed inclusion.

The other thing I would say is, even with the recommendations, everyone who goes through that checkpoint is screened. So when you go through a managed inclusion checkpoint we are screening you with a number of layers of security at that checkpoint and within the airport itself. So I think that is a very important point. Everyone is being screened going through that checkpoint.

Mrs. BROOKS. What happens if the travel documents checker that we have heard referred to misses the selectee marking?

Mr. SADLER. If they miss the selectee marking, that individual is going to be screened. That is the point that I want to make. You don't go through the checkpoint, to my knowledge, without being screened. Whether it is a behavior detection officer, whether it is a canine, whatever, whether it is an ETD, explosion trace detection, those individuals are being screened.

Mrs. BROOKS. I would like to just ask Mr. Piehota, on average, your watch lists, they aren't randomly created. Obviously you get referrals from law enforcement and from others, from FBI, Secret Service, others. How long does it take once an intelligence or a law enforcement agency nominates an individual to make it into the Terrorist Watch List before that person is added to the list?

Mr. PIEHOTA. The time varies due to the complexity of certain issues and the priority assigned to certain watchlisting transactions. Some are routine modifications to records. They are, of course, lower priority rather than people who are added to the list, who receive higher priority. I would not give a specific time period, because it varies from record to record, because there are many different aspects to each record of nomination.

Mrs. BROOKS. Well, and I am certain, having worked with Joint Terrorism Task Forces in the past, when they refer you names, what are some of the criteria that you use to determine how quickly, if the JTTF sends you a name, how quickly does it make it into that list, because, as we know, timing can be critically important in today's environment.

Mr. PIEHOTA. All add nominations are processed immediately. They are usually done, it could be minutes to hours. Modifications, again, the type of modification it is, it could take anywhere from hours to a day or so. If it is a delete action, they generally happen pretty quickly as well, within the next day or so.

Mrs. BROOKS. Mr. Sadler, does TSA have the ability to prevent an individual from boarding an airplane even before that individual is added to a No-Fly List?

Mr. SADLER. Yes. The administrator has the authority to determine who can board an aircraft and who can't.

Mrs. BROOKS. How would that work if TSA believes—maybe it has not yet gone through the practice, they are not on the No-Fly List—how would that process work if TSA receives information that this person should not be boarding a plane?

Mr. SADLER. So based on our earlier comments, the communication between our organizations is as good as I have seen it since I have been in this job. So we would receive that information. If we felt that there was a threat to the aircraft or the risk was too high, then we would notify our vetting operations, who would inhibit the record of that individual, if we had that record, or it would be inhibited when the individual made a reservation, and then we would stop that individual at that point.

Mrs. BROOKS. How often does TSA review the names that are actually on the expedited list?

Mr. SADLER. From the TSC, you mean?

Mrs. BROOKS. Yes. Not from TSC. You have expedited lists. How often does TSA take a look at that list?

Mr. SADLER. We normally do that on a monthly basis, and then I personally review it on a quarterly basis.

Mrs. BROOKS. Okay.

Mr. SADLER. We have a very strict oversight process for that with our chief counsel and with our privacy officer as well when we make those decisions.

Mrs. BROOKS. Thank you. My time is up. I yield back.

Mr. HUDSON. Thank the gentlelady.

The Chairman now recognizes the gentleman from California, Mr. Swalwell, for any questions you may have.

Mr. SWALWELL. Thank you, Chairman.

Last week I had the opportunity, on September 10, to go over to the TSA, Administrator Sadler, you were there, and I met with Administrator Pistole and sat in on your morning threat assessment brief. I appreciate you extending that opportunity to me. It was a very, I think, timely visit, in that September 11 was the next day. I left that meeting impressed with the men and women and the effort behind keeping us safe in the skies every day. So I have great confidence that within our country and across the globe TSA is working hard to make sure we address the evolving threats across the country.

I also believe that the threats that we face right now from ISIL and the way that TSA and DHS are responding is exactly what was envisioned out of the September 11 Commission report. We are certainly being tested today.

Before I ask any further questions, oftentimes it is too easy, I think, for us to beat up on TSA, but I do want to congratulate you on the success so far on PreCheck. I hear about it from my constituents all the time. If anyone hasn't signed up for PreCheck, I really encourage you to sign up for PreCheck. It has been a success. TSA and its partners in implementing it have done a terrific job.

A few questions. First, Director Piehota, your testimony details an extensive system of making sure only the correct individuals are put into the Terrorist Screening Database, but according to Administrator Sadler, 98 percent of the people who ask DHS to remove their names as being incorrectly listed are successful in doing so.

I understand the importance of being over-inclusive. But what assurances can you give us that the TSA as well as DHS are being just as vigorous to put people on that list as they are to take those folks who don't belong on the list off of it? Because it is important to me that that list is accurate. I understand why it has to be a little more broad. But if someone has evidence that they don't belong on the list, I think we need to work overtime to take them off and not inconvenience them. So if you could just briefly explain how the GAO report will bring us to that moment.

Mr. PIEHOTA. Well, in collaboration with our DHS partners, we have cooperatively managed the Redress Inquiry Program. When DHS provides us with an inquiry from their Redress Program, we take it, we make sure that the individual is actually an identical match to an identity in the TSDB. If they have been misidentified, we work with our partners at DHS to expeditiously remove them.

Mr. SWALWELL. Great. Thank you.

I also have a question for Administrator Sadler. In light of the emerging threat from ISIL, the Americans who we know are over there fighting shoulder to shoulder with ISIL, and the thousand-plus Westerners who are in the visa waiver countries, what are we doing right now to ensure that those countries, those visa waiver countries, who do not have 100 percent check against the lost and stolen travel database, the lost and stolen document database, what are we doing with those countries to bring them up to 100 percent compliance?

Mr. SADLER. Yeah. Sir, I can't speak to that. I am not prepared to speak to that today. What I can say, though, is that we work very closely with CBP, Customs and Border Protection, and along with CBP we vet passports against the Stolen and Lost Travel Document database from Interpol. So we are taking actions on our side to try and mitigate that risk and buy the risk down in that area.

Mr. SWALWELL. Great. As we continue to address this threat, is there anything that you believe Congress can do to assist the TSA as we try and learn more about what Americans are over in the Middle East and North Africa? Is there anything that you believe you need additional authority from Congress for or funding to better protect us here at home?

Mr. SADLER. Sir, I mean, we can always use more help, but I think the process that we went through with GAO and the oversight process makes us stronger, because we have somebody who comes in and says, these are the things that we see where you can improve. That is what we are about. We are about buying down risk, we are about getting better every single day so we can do our job the best that we can for the American public.

Mr. SWALWELL. Great. Thank you, Mr. Sadler.

Ms. Grover, thank you for you and your office's helpful report in this matter.

I yield back the balance of my time.

Mr. HUDSON. Thank the gentleman.

The Chairman recognizes the gentleman from South Carolina, Mr. Sanford, for any questions he may have.

Mr. SANFORD. Thank you, Mr. Chairman.

I guess a couple different questions. The first, and I don't mean to be obstinate, but I want to go back to the question that my colleague from New Orleans was asking. It seemed to me like a fairly plain vanilla question, which is, help me understand, if somebody is on the No-Fly List then that means that they can't go and learn how to fly a plane, right?

Mr. SADLER. Yes.

Mr. SANFORD. There were, like, three different bites at the apple, and ultimately still no answer. It was sort-of, if I take you into a dark tunnel, then I can answer the question.

I think from a civil liberties standpoint, that is what drives a lot of people crazy about these different lists that are kept by the Government. If we are a Nation of laws and not men, there is a belief that it ought to be fairly transparent at times where we are coming from. Are you on, are you off? If it takes three cracks at the apple in a public hearing, and then no answer and then the promise of in some closed-door environment we can talk about it, it makes a civil libertarian crazy. So what about that?

Mr. SADLER. Well, sir, I think there are some things that are operationally sensitive that should be discussed within a closed setting. So we try and be as transparent——

Mr. SANFORD. I know. But just going back to common sense, to his point, if you say, let me get this right, you can't go sit in aisle 37D of the airplane, but you can sit in the cockpit, and you can't get an answer on that.

Mr. SADLER. No, sir. I didn't say that.

Mr. SANFORD. No, but you——

Mr. SADLER. I didn't say an individual on a No-Fly List could sit in the cockpit of an aircraft. I didn't say that. What I said was——

Mr. SANFORD. Well, if you learn how to fly an airplane, that is where you are sitting.

Mr. SADLER. What I said was that an individual on the No-Fly List, to my knowledge, has not received training since I have been in this position. All right? What I also said was that there were operationally-sensitive matters that I would like to discuss in a closed session, but I did not say that somebody on the No-Fly List was going to sit in the cockpit. So I want to be very——

Mr. SANFORD. But you also did——

Mr. SADLER. I want to be very clear about that, sir.

Mr. SANFORD. You also equally clearly said that they definitively would—there was no definitive yes or no.

Mr. SADLER. I am telling you, sir, that I do not know of any No-Flys that are sitting in the cockpit of an aircraft. That is as definitive as I can get.

Mr. SANFORD. Okay. Well, that is much more definitive than we got.

Mr. SADLER. When it gets to an operational issue, then I would like to talk to you in a closed session.

Mr. SANFORD. Understood. Okay. All right. We got to a little bit of closure on that one.

Here is another question. I want to follow up on my colleague from California's question with regard to delisting, which again I think is something that would drive somebody from a civil liberties standpoint a bit crazy, which is, you end up on the wrong list, it turns out you shouldn't be on that list. As I understand it now, it is taking people about a year to be cleared from that list, in terms of rough averages, about a year, and that the goal now is to take it down to 3 months. Why does it still take that long?

Mr. SADLER. Well, I want to clarify something. The 98 percent of the individuals that we work with are not on the No-Fly List. They have no nexus to the No-Fly List.

Mr. SANFORD. Understood.

Mr. SADLER. Those are individuals that have been matched potentially to a person who was on the No-Fly List, and then after going through the process you find that they have no nexus to that individual on the watch list. So I just wanted to clarify that.

Ninety-eight percent of the individuals who come through the Redress Program were not on the watch list and taken off; they were individuals that may have been matched to a person on the watch list, and then through our redress process, we determined that they don't have a nexus to the watch list.

Mr. SANFORD. But it is still taking them a year to get off the list.

Mr. SADLER. No. Those cases through the initial redress process, if it is internal to TSA, we can do it within about 2 weeks; if it is external to TSA, so if it is a CBP issue or a Department of State issue, the initial redress takes about 60 days. That is where the majority of those individuals fall, that 98 percent.

Once you get past that point, the other 2 percent, who have some nexus to the watch list, a portion of those may appeal. That is when we start getting into the longer time frame.

Mr. SANFORD. Okay. I guess one question would be, though, even if you are taken off the list, so as I understand it, you are still then on a cleared list.

Mr. SADLER. That is correct, sir.

Mr. SANFORD. Why be on any list at all?

Mr. SADLER. Because we want to give you a redress number that would allow you to enter that into your reservation, so when you come back with another reservation we can run that through our system and we can keep you from being inconvenienced again. It is our way of ensuring that you can go through the checkpoint without being inconvenienced.

Mr. SANFORD. But, I mean, I thought you were cleared. So if you got one citizen who goes through the line, turns out he has never had any mishap, never been on any wrong list, he is not on a cleared list. Why should somebody that went through, turns out they were bungled with somebody else's name, why should they be on again a cleared list, which raises some level of suspicion with regard to, I am on yet another Government list?

Mr. SADLER. Because we are trying to ensure that they can go through the checkpoint without being inconvenienced. So if your name is that close and your date of birth is that close to that individual, the way we clear that name is by assigning this redress control number to the individual that they can put in their reservation and then they should be cleared.

Mr. SANFORD. One last question. Well, I am going over. I guess I can't. Can I ask one more question? Five seconds? No. Okay. Come back to it. Yes, sir.

Mr. HUDSON. I am happy to do a second round if the committee would like to do that.

Mr. SANFORD. Thank you. Yes, sir.

Ms. JACKSON LEE. I yield to him so he can ask his question.

Mr. HUDSON. Well, if the gentlelady is willing to hold off for a second before her start——

Ms. JACKSON LEE. I will.

Mr. HUDSON [continuing]. Then sure, we will allow the gentleman to ask one more question.

Mr. SANFORD. Well, I thank the gentlewoman from Texas. Thank you very much.

I guess my one question would be with all these lists, as I understand it, whether it is a Member of Congress or whether it is anybody in this room, even we are on different levels of risk in terms of gradation. Is that correct?

Mr. SADLER. Well, I wouldn't go gradation. Well, that is a correct answer, but our lists are based on what we know about you.

Mr. SANFORD. Well, my only point being, again from a civil liberties standpoint, whether it is a Member of Congress who has Secret clearance and a whole host of other things, or a member of the military or somebody out here, again, why do they have to be on any gradation with regard to lists? Why couldn't we just clear those folks off this?

Mr. SADLER. Well, we have to know, sir, that when you are coming through the airport that it is you, and we can move you off. That is the whole intent of PreCheck. We want to move those people off that we know so we can focus our resources where they need to be focused.

Mr. SANFORD. But as I am saying, you could be on TSA, have PreCheck, but still have a risk factor assigned to you, and I don't understand that risk factor.

But I have taken too much time from the gentlewoman from Texas and I need to yield back to her. I really appreciate it. Thank you, ma'am.

Mr. HUDSON. Thank the gentleman.

The Chairman now recognizes the gentlelady from Texas, Ms. Jackson Lee, for any questions she may have.

Ms. JACKSON LEE. Mr. Chairman, let me thank you and Mr. Richmond for this hearing, very timely hearing, and following up on the hearings that we have had this week, the briefings that we have had. I just had an opportunity to sit on the Foreign Affairs Committee for the testimony of Secretary Kerry; as he testified in the Senate yesterday, he was in the House today. We had a full committee hearing in the Homeland Security Committee with Mr. Thompson, Mr. McCaul this week. Previously the Border Security and Maritime Security addressed the question of the visa waivers and other ways and means that individuals who may be foreign fighters or who may attempt to come into the United States might use, and so that we must be vigilant to do so.

Certainly the witnesses before us represent the component of vigilance that is important. Secretary Johnson was here, of course, and represented well the position of the Department of Homeland Security.

Let me make one or two points before. We are in a posture of making sure that we coordinate and are aware of the actions that are taken outside the borders of this Nation to protect the homeland and to collaborate with what is done on the soil of the Nation to protect the homeland and the American people. So it is important for the knowledge of the actions that are going to be taken, the train and equip, that Congress is briefed on that. It is well-known by the American people that there have been air strikes, and there are deliberations on the utilization of air strikes in places where ISIL can be stopped. There is collaboration with other nations in a variety of ways. I think it all makes to the security of this Nation.

So I make the point, and I hope that I will make this on the record and that we can get it clarified, on the McKeon amendment establishing the appropriate committees that should be briefed as the actions have taken place on the train and equip, the Homeland Security Committee in both the House and the Senate, I believe, should be added. It is outrageous that the drafters of the amendment left out the Homeland Security Committee. It would be good to keep it quiet and not let anyone know that they have been left out, but I believe that it is an egregious error by the drafters and whoever is responsible and that there is no way that you can ensure the safety of the homeland unless we are collaborating. So I hope someone hears it and I hope someone makes a correction on that point.

The second point I want to do is to encourage my colleagues to join me on the legislation that I have introduced, the No-Fly Foreign Fighters legislation, which does not compromise a recent court case dealing with the watch lists and the No-Fly structure that I understand was just rendered. This is a simple cleaning-up. The language I think that is relevant in this legislation that has been introduced is that the terrorist watch lists utilized by the Transportation Security Administration, to determine basically if this is a complete list. So we are asking for the appropriate agencies to determine whether or not this list that is being utilized is an accurate list, is a complete list. It has no impact on one's removal. That process is being reviewed. I agree with the American Civil Liberties Union that there should be a proper process for removal. But I hope my colleagues will join in this, simple, that says no fly for foreign fighters. I will read some of the language in a moment.

I see my time is out. So let me just, if I could, ask this question, and maybe you will answer it, to—is it Mr. Piehota? Is that the correct pronunciation?

Mr. PIEHOTA. Yes.

Ms. JACKSON LEE. As I indicated, we held a recent hearing on the Visa Waiver Program, and during that hearing concerns were expressed that someone with a passport from a Western country that has joined in the fighting in Syria or in any other place in the region where there are efforts at jihad, joined with a terrorist organization, could be only one flight away from our shores.

On Tuesday I introduced the No-Fly for Foreign Fighters Act. Are individuals known to have joined terrorist organizations in

Syria and Iraq, is there seemingly a current list or current knowledge of those individuals, and are they being placed in a position not to possibly do harm in to the United States and to the American people? Are we continually updating and making sure that we have a complete list to address?

Then my other subset of that, to explain to the subcommittee how Secure Flight is being used to identify passengers flying internationally for enhanced screening based on risk-based, intelligence-driven information.

Mr. PIEHOTA. The Terrorist Screening Database is updated on a 24-hour, 7-day-a-week basis through collaboration with the law enforcement, homeland security, and intelligence communities. We do this in partnership, we do this in a joint National security mission fashion.

The Terrorist Screening Database at the current time has approximately 9,000 identities that have been associated with foreign terrorist fighter activities. Of those 9,000 identities, 95 percent of these people have already been watchlisted at the No-Fly level.

Ms. JACKSON LEE. On the Secure——

Mr. PIEHOTA. That information is then transmitted in a transactional real-time fashion to our TSA partners, who then use it in their Secure Flight program.

Ms. JACKSON LEE. So let me just conclude, Mr. Chairman, by saying, and the idea of my legislation is for Congress to be advised on the completeness of the Terrorist Screening Database, which I think has not been done, particularly to our relevant committees, and to ensure that it is continuously updated, and particularly with those who have gone for the fight.

So I hope my colleagues will consider the legislation, but I thank the gentleman. I reinforce the point that I am making with this legislation, but as well with the questions that I asked, in order to secure the homeland, the committees of jurisdiction that are relevant to the actions outside of the boundaries of this Nation must collaborate with those who have the ultimate responsibility for the securing of this Nation. As I understand it, that is the jurisdiction of the Homeland Security Committee and in this instance on the aviation and other matters with the Transportation Security Committee. I hope we can fix this as quickly as possible.

With that, Mr. Chairman, I yield back.

Mr. HUDSON. Well, I thank the gentlelady.

Thank the witnesses for your testimony and all of the Members for your questions today.

The Members of the subcommittee may have additional questions for the witnesses we will ask that you respond to in writing.

Without objection, the subcommittee stands adjourned. Thank you.

[Whereupon, at 3:17 p.m., the subcommittee was adjourned.]

APPENDIX

QUESTION FROM HONORABLE MICHAEL D. ROGERS FOR STEPHEN SADLER

Question. The Secure Flight Program's success depends in large part upon supporting contracts and contractors. Please provide an overview and status update on each of the TSA's supporting Secure Flight and Operational Computing Environment contracts and acquisitions, including the length and cost of each contract.

Answer. The Transportation Security Administration's Secure Flight contract information requested is provided in the tables below:

Active Contract No.	Contract Type	Contractor	Description of Supply/Service	Period of Performance (Start & End Date)	Total Value $ Million
1	Cost Plus Fixed Fee (CPFF).	Flatter & Associates.	Independent validation & verification services.	Sep 18, 2009 thru Mar 17, 2015.	7.049
2	CPFF	Infozen	System operations & maintenance, production environment.	Feb 1, 2008 thru Nov 27, 2014.	64.779
3	Firm Fixed Price (FFP).	InfoGlide	Bladeworks software maintenance.	Jan 4, 2011 thru Nov 3, 2015.	9.391
4	Time and Material (T&M).	IBM	System application development and Tier 3 Support.	Dec 14, 2013 thru Oct 20, 2014.	16.837
5	FFP	Comp Sci Corp.	WebEOC support.	Nov 1, 2013 thru Aug 3, 2015.	0.251
6	FFP	Dell	Hardware	Dec 17, 2013 thru Dec 16, 2014.	0.292
7	FFP	Infozen	Hardware/Software (H/W) maintenance renewal, H/S license, spare parts.	Apr 1, 2013 thru Nov 27, 2014.	6.974
8	FFP	Omniplex	Physical Security.	Nov 10, 2013 thru Nov 9, 2018.	1.813
9	FFP	TSA Office of Facilities.	Annapolis Junction facility lease and utilities.	Oct 22, 2013 thru Jan 31, 2018.	13.616
10	FFP	TSA Office of Facilities.	Colorado Springs facility lease and utilities.	Oct 22, 2013 thru Dec 21, 2018.	9.286

Active Con- tract No.	Contract Type	Contractor	Description of Supply/Service	Period of Performance (Start & End Date)	Total Value $ Million
11	FFP	Customs and Border Protection.	Connectivity with Customs and Border Protection.	Aug 11, 2009 thru Aug 10, 2015.	15.254
12	Labor Hour (LH).	RCM Solutions.	Program management support.	Apr 9, 2010 thru Jan 12, 2015.	4.862
13	LH	SRA	Privacy program development and support.	Sep 21, 2009 thru Mar 20, 2015.	4.206
14	CPFF	Deloitte Consulting.	Implementation and business operations.	Aug 11, 2012 thru Jan 31, 2015.	18.722
15	FFP	GSA	Lines connectivity.	July 1, 2014 thru June 30, 2015.	0.589
16	FFP	Zibiz Corp.	Hardware	Mar 23, 2012 thru Mar 21, 2015.	1.900
17	FFP	Immix- technology.	Software license	Apr 1, 2013 thru Mar 31, 2015.	0.011
18	FFP	ECS Gov, Inc.	Software	Dec 20, 2011 thru Mar 31, 2016.	2.959
19	FFP	Snap, Inc.	Virtual Storage, Smart Cloud.	Sep 22, 2014 thru Sep 21, 2015.	1.028
20	FFP	Govplace	Net App SAN (storage).	Sep 19, 2014 thru Sep 18, 2015.	0.229
21	FFP	ESC Gov (IBM).	Enterprise license agreement.	April 15, 2013 thru Mar 31, 2018.	61.100
22	FFP	Dell	Software license	Apr 1, 2013 thru Mar 31, 2014.	0.089
23	CPFF	QinetiQ North America.	System operations and maintenance —under protest.	July 15, 2013 thru Oct 31, 2014.	9.481
24	FFP	Govplace	Software	April 1, 2014 thru March 31, 2015.	0.041
25	T&M	Sev1tech, Inc.	Implementation and business operations.	Nov 17, 2014 thru June 20, 2018.	14.912
26	T&M	IBM	System development and Tier 3 System Support.	Aug 20, 2014 thru Feb 19, 2016.	34.458
27	FFP	Wildflower	DBI Data Base software.	Sep 10, 2014 thru Sep 9, 2015.	0.121

○